Praise for The Qui

CW00815986

"Beautifully and engagingly writter
life is especially moving. Stagg refle
the extraordinary characters he ha
transformation. What he offers is n
room for all of us to see how amazing grace can work in our lives, too."

– Richard Leonard SJ
author of *Where the hell is God?*

"The nonviolent Jesus once confessed to his friends that he was 'gentle and humble of heart.' That, we might say, is the spiritual life in a nutshell. Here, Cormac Stagg shares his own spiritual journey to the God of universal love and compassion. His testimony invites us to take another step forward on our own journeys, to surrender completely to God, and to welcome the gift of 'a gentle and humble heart.' If we heed Cormac's lessons of the heart, then perhaps we might disarm and create a gentler, more loving, peaceful world."

– Rev. John Dear
author of *Living Peace, The Questions of Jesus,
The Nonviolent Life, and The Beatitudes of Peace*

"Stagg bravely lays his heart bare to show us the profound cracks in it that let the light in. His is an engrossing testament in praise of ongoing spiritual surrender. Because as he illustrates, beyond the ego-self and its ruinous deceptions awaits an all-embracing Love. Stagg carefully affirms, there are many ways to approach this Spirit-infused, liberating space of grace. Yet, through his own dramatic journey, we recognize that before one can hope to fly, we must drop to their knees and learn to crawl."

– Yahia Lababidi
author of *Quarantine Notes: Aphorisms on Morality & Mortality*

"The Quest for a Humble Heart is an uplifting story of recovery, redemption, and hope. Stagg is a master storyteller, as well as a rare and precious repository of humility, humor, and wisdom."

– Warren Ward
author of *Lovers of Philosophy: How the Intimate Lives
of Seven Philosophers Shaped Modern Thought*

When the heart gets changed,
everything changes.

THE QUEST FOR A HUMBLE HEART

A PATH TO INNER PEACE & FREEDOM

CORMAC STAGG

Mercy River Publishing
Owen Stanly Pl, Darra, Qld 4076, Australia

Design by Jacqui Lynch, Preloaded Design.

ISBN: 978-0-6457066-0-4

First published in 2023.

A catalogue record for this
book is available from the
National Library of Australia

Contents

INTRODUCTION

A while ago, I wrote a poem, a rhymed narrative called "God's Eyes," as an ode to a man I had encountered twenty-five years earlier. I had been taking calls on a 12-step helpline and received a call from a woman in Sydney, Australia. She had a relative housed in an aged-care facility some 500 miles away in Brisbane. Given my location, she wanted to know if someone would spend a little time with this old man, who she suspected was approaching the end of his life.

She explained that though his early years had been decidedly colorful, he had straightened out his life with the help of others with equally misspent pasts. In fact, Ron assisted many others like himself before eventually succumbing to a stroke, which left him mostly paralyzed and unable to speak. I was to learn that he had survived in that circumstance for over two decades without saying a single word, unable to walk or care for himself.

I vividly recall my first encounter with Ron. There was something truly startling about his eyes. They were piercingly blue, discerning, and intelligent. As I have often said, they were the most beautiful blue eyes I'd ever seen on a man. I knew in an instant—let's call it intuitive knowledge—that whatever else his stroke had taken from him (and it had taken much!), he still had complete clarity of thought. But more than that, he had something one sometimes encounters among people who have walked the long mile. Ron had discernible wisdom and an almost audible peace. That was it; I was hooked, and we became the perfect couple: me, a fella with a truckload of his own demons to share who couldn't stop talking, and him, the quintessential perfect listener with those eyes that seemed to know all, accept all, and strangely, even absolve all. God's eyes, which spoke from the heart.

Of course, this happy union could not continue forever, and the day arrived when I was told that Ron's time on this Earth was all but done. The news of his impending demise tied knots in my usually fluent tongue. So, as I sat with him that fateful day, I twisted verbally this way and that trying to find some words of comfort. Ultimately, after several stumbling, inelegant attempts, I said something like, "Although someone like me could not know for sure, perhaps whatever happens next might not be too bad. Maybe, just maybe, there might not be too much to fear."

He held me in his gentle gaze throughout this awkward and seemingly endless ramble. Then, as easily as the most practiced baritone, his muted tongue, which had not uttered a word for decades, spoke. He said, "I know." To say that every inch of me both then and now believes that I was witness to the miraculous is really all I can offer. Struck dumb myself but curiously comforted, I left him for the last time, at least for a while. Within an hour, I received the news that he had gone wherever indeed we go.

I wept from the heart that day over the loss of this God-infused man. For surely, I thought, I had those past few months been sitting in the company of a son of God, an embodied spirit, or as a friend of mine likes to say, "God with skin on." Yet our happy liaisons had little or nothing to do with our shared holiness. Rather, they had everything to do with our shared brokenness, both past and present.

Years later, and with the benefit of a theology degree, nearly two decades of Ignatian meditation practice, and an ongoing commitment to my Catholic faith, I am more convinced than ever that it was the God from below, the inside-out, upside-down, last-is-first God that I encountered during those months with Ron. The God proclaimed by a Jewish itinerant holy man from Galilee, whom renowned Oxford scholar Geza Vermes called a Galilean Hasid,[1] and whose insistent teaching about that selfsame God who favors the poor, lame, mute, and utterly disdained saw him nailed to a cross.

This little chip of a book is not a theological thesis or an attempt to uphold or argue for or against any specific religious persuasion or belief. Such efforts, where they are useful, are best undertaken by those more qualified than I. Neither will its contents hold much sway with those God-seekers who prefer a neatly defined, well-packaged God of doctrinal certainty. God alone knows there is no shortage of offerings from those blowing a trumpet, with unabashed certitude, for this or that version of the one true faith. Rather, by necessity and intent, these chapters are about the spirituality of the

---

1   Geza Vermes, *Jesus the Jew: A Historian's Reading of the Gospels* (London: Collins, 1973). See Chapter Fifteen.

heart—the path to inner peace and freedom—with all its implied inclusivity. This is, to be sure, a sometimes-wild ride toward an intimate, ongoing, practical experience of God that is absolutely game-changing, earthbound, and entirely accessible by anyone.

The central claim of this book, and the spiritual foundation on which it rests, is that the living God is ever-present, radically inclusive, and is the manifestation of pure love and compassion.[2] St. Augustine famously said, "Our hearts are restless till they find rest in thee." A thousand years later, a wacky mystic called Ignatius of Loyola spoke about finding God in all things. This book is about that search, a trek of a restless heart—a journey that I believe is completely open to everyone.

If there is a criterion of any sort for taking this long walk—one that I am still on, albeit with many missteps, it is that along the way, an embrace of humility as a way of being becomes essential, and the practice of radically other-centered inclusive love becomes an imperative. That's what my disabled, mute man was like; indeed, that's what the living God that I eventually came to know is like! The One whose promise was and is that divisions of ethnicity, gender, class, wealth, and religion cannot hold in an upturned world of the Spirit—a world infused with that same God who is ever-present love. A world where patriarchy crumbles on its own decrepit foundations, and power, prestige, and money are a distinct liability. This is a story about the journey toward that God, a mysterious God for sure, who defies complete

---

2   The descriptor of the living God as love and compassion is used repeatedly throughout this book and is explained theologically in Chapter Fifteen.

definition but is, I believe, as close as our next breath and whispers gently through the unfettered imagination to everyone who seeks the humble-hearted place. *For when the heart gets changed, everything changes!*

CHAPTER ONE

WHEN THE STUDENT IS READY

Not everyone needs to be brought low, shaken and stirred, or reduced to a state of powerlessness and despair to embark on the spiritual journey, the quest for a humble heart. But folks of my ilk are usually averse to giving up on their former ways just because it's getting a little hot in the kitchen. In fact, whether it is from self-deception, dogged determination, or a combination of both, people like me will simply never give in until not just the kitchen but the whole house has gone up in flames. At least for some of us, becoming ready is no small, quick, or easy task. In my case, it took half a lifetime.

I am one of six sons. I was born in Ireland but raised in England from the age of six. My brothers and I experienced what I suspect is common to any first-generation migrant family from anywhere in the world. We straddled two worlds: the one at home, which was as Irish as one could wish, and the one outside, which was a rather well-to-do, genteel English country town. Irish people hold their heritage close, and this remains true for me to this day. To say that we stood out is to understate it. An enormous family by English standards, with strange names and odd accents to boot, we soon grew accustomed to regular xenophobic slurs and worse, none of which was ever taken lying down.

To add insult to injury, at least as I saw it, my father's low wage meant we were relatively poor compared to many around us. Of course, these were the perceptions of a boy. Realistically, we never wanted for anything. But turning up for school until my early teens with haircuts administered by my mother that would not have been out of place on a Franciscan monk did little to help matters. Nor did the ill-fitting school uniforms, cast off by their original wearers. Nor did the time two of us got bundled off on a poor-boys holiday, which turned out to be more like a living hell, about as close to prison boot camp as you can get. Neither did the line-up for school lunches do much to dampen my grievances, as those of us getting lunch for free had different colored lunch tickets. They might just as well have tattooed "poor kids" on our foreheads.

By the time I was fifteen, I had a rebel streak running right through me. Not, I might add, uncommon in my family or among my compatriots. I had developed a loathing for the British class system and all its connotations and an equal disdain for anyone in authority. These traits did little to assist me with my education, which had been decidedly rudimentary and ended as soon as I turned sixteen. As I walked out those school gates for the last time, I had two abiding convictions, coupled with a fierce determination. First, I would be a servant to no man, and second, I would do whatever it took not to be poor.

It would be another two decades before I saw that the problem was not external; it was and is an internal issue of self-centered pride, coupled with various other manifestations of what a famous, sober, ex-boozehound named Bill Wilson called "the bondage of self."[3]

I took an apprenticeship learning how to shoe horses but not because that was what I wanted to do. Certainly, I had a great love of riding and caring for horses. I had been doing that with other people's horses since I was a small boy. My dream was to become a jockey, but a brief stint in a world-renowned racing stable soon revealed that, though I was a little skinny guy, I was too big for that gig. However, my self-imposed rebellious trap had already been set. Although I would have been much better suited to taking up the skills of a groom or stable lad, I just could not countenance doffing my cap to anyone, especially the folks who employ horsemen and horsewomen. While too big to be a jockey, I didn't possess the size and strength to be a farrier. But I had my ace card: that fierce determination. Yes, I could push through. Whatever it took, I'd never be poor, and I'd be a servant to no one. And here was a skill I thought could guarantee both of these essentials.

As a child, they called me willful. Much later, in an entirely different sort of business in Australia, I became known as a tenacious bastard, a badge I wore with a great deal of pride. By that time, I certainly wasn't poor. Indeed, I was looking like a fella who might make a big wad of cash, a fella who

3   Bill Wilson, *Alcoholics Anonymous: The Story of How Many Thousands of Men and Women Have Recovered from Alcoholism,* 4th rev. ed. (New York: Alcoholics Anonymous World Services, 2001), 62-63.

would be no one's servant. My iron will, my self-sufficiency, and my innate determination appeared to have served me well. I had succeeded in everything I turned my hand to since walking out of those school gates.

But by now I had developed what some friends of mine call the "disease of more"—more of this, more of that, more of everything. Enough was never nearly enough. I remember when I first rubbed shoulders with some seriously successful businesspeople. It completely baffled me why they kept working, often very hard, when they could have been off somewhere enjoying their millions. Later I understood that the drive for success in this world is not just about the money; it's the insatiable desire of the ego for power and prestige.

However, in my little world, serious cracks now appeared. The kitchen was getting warm. This certainly prompted genuine concern from my then-wife, a truly wonderful woman, business partner, and the best mother in the world to our two sons. She endured much along the way and ultimately became my ex-wife, one of the many losses that were now ahead of me on my journey to become ready.

I knew at some level that all was not well, but any form of introspection, spiritual or otherwise, was for weaklings. The growing darkness within me I would overcome without saying a word about it to a living soul. After all, I could push through. Pushing through was my thing. I was a guy who did not, could not, fail. St. Paul writes, "When I am weak, then I am strong" (2 Cor 12:10). But I was still a series of devastating defeats away from comprehending what a statement like that might mean.

Increasingly disenchanted with my circumstances, I entered a realm, at least in my hidden imaginings, where delusions of grandeur became the norm. Yes, a fella like me must surely be destined for still greater things—things that would ensure once and for all that I'd never be a servant or poor. Around this time, an experienced entrepreneur and close friend approached me with a potential business idea that we could progress together. It was a new franchise being developed in the United States. Did I want to go over, have a look, and then report back? Could this be my next great venture? I thought it probably could, so off I went.

Greed and avarice thinly disguised as "Oh, well, that's just business" are not the bedfellows of all businesspeople, especially the good ones. But these traits certainly had a hold on me. By day three in the US, I had cut my friend of many years standing out of the deal and was busy negotiating a license for the whole of the UK for myself. I returned to Australia and bullied and cajoled my very dubious wife into agreeing that we should dispose of two of our best assets. I then duly dispatched the proceeds, a sizable sum, to the US. We never heard from them again. How foolish the deluded can be. It turned out that this was a well-executed scam that had duped businesspeople not only in the US but also from various other parts of the world. To say I was devastated is an understatement. To say my recklessness appalled my wife equally so. Twelve months later, I was off and running again on yet another 'Let's make Cormac richer and more powerful' venture. Another great frolic of grandiosity that did not end well.

In retrospect, I now realize that I had probably been suffering from clinical depression for an extended period—not helped by the copious amount of alcohol that I had been consuming for years, which had, let's just say, become a problem. My iron will, my push through, and my "never surrender to anyone or anything under any circumstances" (which may have been helpful to me years earlier) had now become a ragged road to ruin. This time I drove us right over a financial cliff, and we lost all our money and a rather large slice of my mother-in-law's money as well. Soon afterward, I reluctantly received a diagnosis of depression. However, I couldn't or wouldn't completely accept it.

All my circumstances now dictated that I was a guy who should have experienced at least some sense of humility. But prideful ego is a fearsome thing that does not vanish in a twinkling, if ever. And I still believed that it was only a matter of time before riches and glory days would be mine again. After all, surely it was not my destiny to be poor and a servant to others. A couple of years later, an opportunity did present itself when a newly elected member of parliament employed me to work as a junior staffer in her office. Of course, that is not how I saw myself, and within twelve months, she had grown tired of my self-promotion and egocentric blather, and she sacked me.

After my dismissal, my wife and I finally separated. I left that marriage with little more than I had when we met twenty years earlier—the clothes on my back and a banged-up old car. A friend invited me to stay with him for a couple of weeks while I got myself sorted. It wouldn't be long, I thought. A fella like me! I'd soon be living again in fine style, an inner-city bachelor pad perhaps, with all of its associated connotations. Of course, I didn't have a job, had hardly any income, and virtually no prospects in either of these areas. But, hey, this was me. Something would happen; it wouldn't be long. I mean, a fella like me—I'd soon be back in the main game better than ever!

Chapter Two

Rude Awakening

As I entered the suburb where my friend lived, I had an acute awareness that this was strange territory for me. This was one of those areas where the poor people live, an area that I had hitherto avoided. Every second house I drove past seemed in serious need of refurbishment, if not outright demolition. And what was it about these guys, I wondered, that compelled nearly all of them to have not one but two or three huge killer dogs barely contained behind dubious fences?

My friend's house was at the lower end of the scale, even by these unflattering standards. It was tiny and dilapidated, built who knows when, and so close to the railroad tracks that as the trains roared by—which they did 24/7—the entire place would shake. My generous friend showed me to my threadbare room, where there was an old single bed that had seen better days. I recall that it all seemed quite surreal. How could this have happened? I, who was never, ever, under any circumstance going to be poor, was now thrust among them. But, hey, a fella like me, surely this was only a temporary aberration? Give it a couple of weeks, and something would happen. I mean, hey, a fella like me!

Eight years later, I was still there! And I would be to this day except that the place got sold and I had to move out. Today, I thank God for those years in such humble surroundings, for it was during that time that I finally became ready. I was to learn that not only was I among the poor, but I was one of the poorest among them.

It is not incidental that the Galilean Hasid repeatedly emphasizes poverty as a spiritual precondition for entering what he called the kingdom of Heaven.[4] Or, to put it another way, only the humble-hearted can be in full relationship with the living God, who is compassion and love personified.

It is not my intention, however, to imply that material poverty should be in any way glorified. Indeed, justice for the poor is, without doubt, a primary biblical narrative.[5] Rather, what I am trying to convey is a condition of the heart, a heart sufficiently humbled that it can commune with God. Because *it is precisely in the "language of the heart" that God communes.*

Material poverty is thus neither a guarantee nor necessarily a precondition for the quest for inner peace with purpose. One of my greatest spiritual teachers and someone I have

---

4 Numerous sayings of Jesus emphasize the need for humility or poverty of spirit. It is this rather than material poverty that is crucial. See Chapter Sixteen.

5 All the Hebrew prophets, including Jesus, condemn inequality and the consequent exploitation of the poor. This is further explained in Chapters Thirteen and Fifteen.

walked with for a quarter of a century is a man of great wealth. His path to a humble heart—and he is one of the humblest men I have ever known—was no less arduous than my own. Indeed, it may have been more so, specifically because all his wealth was still in place. However, for someone like me, being brought low materially was a necessary part of the journey *because the two things that I had run so hard from throughout my life—poverty and being a servant to others—were what I needed to embrace most.*

But I did not magically wake up on my first morning in my new humble surroundings and arrive at any of the above insights. I had a way to go; I was still not ready. A brief period of employment soon followed, but true to form, I was thinking about power, prestige, and money, lots of money. This came to an abrupt halt after being dismissed from that job as well. This time it wasn't because of my prideful, grandiose tendencies but because I was well and truly crippled with depression. If I had harbored doubts about my depression some years earlier, these were about to be ravaged, and so was I.

The dark nights of the soul that followed were excruciating. Everything that I believed about myself was being utterly demolished and placed into a dark void, from which I became increasingly convinced there was no return! I battled with everything I had, only to be beaten into submission again and again. I cursed myself for the weakling I had become. Where was my determination, my push-through, my never-surrender? Even shaving in the morning required an effort that I frequently could not muster. I couldn't face anyone or anything. The simplest task seemed insurmountable—and what was the point, anyway? I was a done deal, broken, useless.

As weeks like this grew into months, I prayed to be taken from this living hell in my sleep. And when that didn't happen, I seriously considered more affirmative means of achieving the same result. As I sit writing these words, I am acutely aware of the large number of people every year who take their own lives. Indeed, I might well have been among them were it not for the tragic loss of a young man I stumbled upon one Saturday morning.

In the midst of all this darkness, I received a call from my ex-wife. Her mother was seriously ill in another part of Australia. She needed to go immediately to be by her side, and she needed me to come and stay at the family home and care for our two boys until she returned. There is nothing in this world that I love more than my two boys. But caring for them seemed impossible in my utterly broken state. I also had real misgivings about my lads seeing me in that condition. However, pride is a double-edged sword because I also didn't want to admit, especially to my ex-wife, that I was incapable. I would like to claim a nobler motive for going, but it was my old buddy pride that got me out there. Or perhaps it was fate.

My care for my lads was rough and ready. I fed them after a fashion, but other than that, I was mostly confined to a lounge chair, either reading or sleeping. Mercifully, so far as I could tell, they seemed blissfully unaware of my internal turmoil and just got on with doing their own thing the way lads do. And so, it came to pass early on a Saturday morning. I thought I'd try to walk the dog. My ex-wife's home is a beautiful property on the rural outskirts of Brisbane. Just a short walk from her front door and the dog and I were in an open landscape of fields and woodland.

As soon as I saw a stationary car in the distance, I knew that something was badly amiss. It was, you might say, in the wrong place at the wrong time—parked at the end of a lonely track at the bottom of a field, just after dawn. The hairs on the back of my neck started sounding an alarm. As I got closer, I could see that there was somebody in the car. Okay, I thought, could be just someone sleeping off a big Friday night, but how in hell did they find this completely isolated spot? Closer still and I noticed an odd mist or haze within the car. Now I'm there. Yes, there is a young man in the back seat, apparently asleep. Should I just keep walking? No. Every instinct in me was now at play. I felt compelled to open the car door, which I duly did when tapping on the widow failed to wake him. But there would be no waking for this poor soul. As I stepped back in shock from my gruesome discovery, I could now see a large hose attached to the car exhaust. This young man had taken his own life.

It was what my mother used to call a "rude awakening." I remember the matter-of-fact way the police went about assessing the situation. Without doubt, they were professionals, but there was something more than professionalism at work here. This was a scene, I realized, that they were all too familiar with— one of the many suicides that police routinely investigate. I recall that I couldn't stop crying as I gave the police my statement. This tragedy shook me to the core. What I didn't say to the police was all too apparent to me—that this young man had acted on what I had been contemplating. I knew nothing about him or the journey that had led him to that dark lonesome track. But I knew everything about the terrible internal, soul-destroying darkness that he must have been feeling because I felt it too. It was as if he were me and

I were him. The implications were stark. I was finally ready!

As I later pondered the horror of that morning, I thought of his family. There was a world of pain coming their way, a level of sorrow and grief that would probably never subside. Suicide is like a tsunami: it's not always unexpected, but very often it is. Either way, when it happens, the level of destruction that it leaves in its wake is beyond imagining: his mother and father, his siblings, if he had them; the guilt, the questioning, what could have they done differently? If only this or that.

Then it hit me like a hammer blow. Was he married like me, separated like me? Oh, my god, did he have two wonderful boys as I had? In that moment, the self-destructive delusions of my depression lifted sufficiently for me to see the insanity of where my mind had been taking me. He was me, and I was him. I wept from the heart; I was ready! And as the old adage would have it, *when the student is ready, the teacher will appear.* Or, in my case, teachers.

Before moving on to discuss this next phase of the journey, there is a crucial rider that I want to insert. Nothing that follows suggests that a spiritual path, however vigorously practiced, negates the need for accessing good and ongoing medical help to treat depression. The notion that God will somehow magically cure an illness like depression, bypassing the need for human health care, is grossly ill-informed and dangerous. Indeed, a central pillar of this book is that there is no medical care or anything else that is good in this world that does not have the One who is loving and compassionate intimately woven in and through it. To put it simply, God works through all of Creation, including people.

My most enduring spiritual teacher—the humble, rich fella referred to previously—helped me to see how spiritual pride can block acceptance of God's modus operandi on Earth. As we sat talking one day, he told me a story:

> There was a man, a fella of great faith. He took himself up a high mountain one day because the mighty flood was coming. Unconcerned even as the water reached his ankles, he assured himself that God would save him, for, after all, he was a man of great faith. As the water continued to rise to his waist, suddenly a boat appeared, and the people on the boat called out to him, "We will save you." "No need," said he. "I am a man of great faith; God will save me." Before long, the water was up to his chest, and suddenly a helicopter appeared, and the crew on board called out to him, "We will save you." "Don't bother," said he, "I am a man of great faith; God will save me." A short time later, he drowned, and when he got to Heaven, he was furious with God: "How could you let this happen? I'm a man of great faith," he thundered! Then God said, "I sent you a boat and a helicopter."

Depression is a merciless killer. In my case, it has also been a great humbler. But the life-changing spiritual transformation of the heart is never a solitary adventure and must always include embracing the boats and helicopters that God sends our way. Human mental health measures and pursuing a spiritual life are not mutually exclusive; they are entirely complementary.

CHAPTER THREE

MYSTICS, MISFITS, AND REALLY BAD BOYS

If there was any relief to be had during those long months of despairing darkness in that ramshackle, barren, train-shaken old house, it was that I could escape momentarily into some other world by reaching for a book. Reading helped me drift into sleep and get some relief from the darkness.

By the time I encountered the tragic loss of the young man outlined in the previous chapter, I had read the accounts by various people of their spiritual quests. I read Bede Griffiths' autobiography of his path from Oxford scholar to Benedictine monk[6] and learned that he subsequently spent decades living in abject poverty in India. Indeed, he eventually became a fully-fledged Indian swami. I read a book called *The Wounded Healer,* by Henri Nouwen,[7] who was no

---

6   Bede Griffiths, *The Golden String: An Autobiography* (Springfield, Illinois: Templegate Publishers, 1954, 1980).

7   Henri J. M. Nouwen, *The Wounded Healer: Ministry in Contemporary Society* (New York: Image Books Doubleday, 1972).

stranger to the ravages of depression. He left a comfortable and prestigious position as a professor at Harvard Divinity School and spent the rest of his life living and working with people with intellectual and developmental disabilities at the L'Arche Daybreak Community in Ontario.

I found myself also curiously drawn by some of the sayings of the wacky, out-there misfits and mystics who became known as the Desert Fathers, the earliest exemplars of Christian monasticism. "Desert Fathers" is an unfortunate patriarchal descriptor because many of these ascetics were, in fact, Desert Mothers. Indeed, some of the best-loved sayings of these mystics came from the women, who also held leadership positions in these isolated, countercultural, third- and fourth-century communities.[8]

Wacky and out-there, oh, yes; these are my kind of folk. Speaking of which, I also read a biography of St. Francis of Assisi. Here was someone who, a thousand years after the Desert Mothers and Fathers, would not have been out of place among them. Born into a wealthy family, he abandoned it all in his pursuit of a humble heart, a heart like the Galilean whom he insisted on trying to emulate. Francis' trials and tribulations would be many, but spiritually his story is nothing if not inspiring. Sometimes quickly and sometimes slowly, he pared away every vestige of the delusions of the ego-self. Ultimately, what emerged was a Christlike figure, God with skin on, who practiced and spoke only of love.

I also read and listened to accounts of more contemporary figures, including the life of perhaps the greatest American

8   Rowan Williams, *Silence and Honey Cakes: The Wisdom of the Desert* (Oxford: Lion Books, 2003).

who has ever lived, Martin Luther King Jr. I marveled at his oratory. Something deep within me moves when I listen to his "I have a dream" speech. His "I've been to the mountaintop" speech a few years later, in 1968, just before his assassination, is no less extraordinary. By that time, King was under considerable pressure and receiving sustained public criticism from many of his own black brethren. The reason for their consternation was that King would not desist from advocating for poor whites just as vigorously as he did for oppressed people of color. "I've seen the promised land," said King prophetically. If there is a better piece of spiritual oratory than this speech, it's hard to find. King wanted not just black folk but all folk—even poor, white racist folk—in the spiritual tent together. A short time later, it was one of these poor white racists who gunned him down.

It enthralled me to learn that this African American champion of civil rights, a full-on Southern Baptist preacher, had been greatly influenced by the nonviolent Hindu spirituality of Mahatma Gandhi.[9] No less intriguing is that Gandhi partly attributed his nonviolent approach to oppression to the example and teaching of a rule-breaking, non-conformist Jewish mystic and Galilean Hasid that Christians call the Christ. Gandhi writes:

> Though I cannot claim to be a Christian in the sectarian sense, the example of Jesus' suffering is a factor in the composition of my undying faith in non-violence, which rules all my actions, worldly and temporal.[10]

---

9   Mary Elizabeth King, *Mahatma Gandhi and Martin Luther King Jr: The Power of Nonviolent Action, Cultures of Peace* (Paris: UNESCO Publishing, 1999).

10   Mohandas K. Gandhi, *The Collected Works of Mahatma Gandhi,* vol. 31 (New Delhi: Government of India Publications, 1961).

This is glad tidings indeed—an enduring example that God's desire for nonviolent action for oppressed people everywhere knows no limitation. Certainly not those imposed by human-erected religious boundaries.

Martin Luther King Jr., Gandhi, and the Galilean, what a team! All three are extraordinary, and each would pay the ultimate price because they fearlessly pursued a vision of God's desire for a world in which oppression of any sort is a non-starter. They knew that oppression finds its antecedents in prideful elitism, whether it be of race, class, nation, or religion, or some combination of them. King's assassination was an act of race-hate violence but was also inextricably linked to the justice positions that he championed and the religious views that drove his political activism. Twenty years earlier, Gandhi met the same fate, though not at the behest of the imperial power in whose side he had become such a thorn (although they may have considered it). It was at the hands of a fellow Hindu who could not accept his overt tolerance toward Muslims.

When it comes to casting the first violent stone, fellow religionists, whatever their hue, are all too often first past the post. These folks—usually men—are devoid of the ethics of inclusion and grow ever more eager to rid themselves of the rule-breaking misfits who can't or won't hold the elitist line. Two thousand years after the Galilean's death, theologians are still arguing about whether it was the Romans or his fellow Jews who were most responsible. Probably in his case, both state oppressor and elitist religionists had skin in the game. They both wanted him gone, albeit for different reasons.

But at the time I was doing this reading, I certainly wasn't joining the dots in this way. As mentioned, my reading was largely a distraction from my ever-present darkness. Of course, I had heard of some of these folks. Who hasn't?

Regarding the Galilean, it had been many moons since I'd given him or his presumed Father even a passing nod. I am old enough to be from perhaps the last generation for whom being Irish and Catholic were more or less synonymous, a cultural phenomenon that no longer exists in the Ireland of today. Therefore, some vestiges of the old religion that I received as a boy still lingered as I approached the nadir of my brokenness. My parents had ensured, soon after we arrived in England in the 1960s, that my brothers and I received vigorous training in the one true faith. God forbid that any of us should fall victim to the influences of those English Protestants.

However, for someone like me who had fallen afoul of much of what I thought the old faith professed, this was cold comfort. As children, we had received many diatribes about a punishing god, an old white fella with a beard, off in Heaven somewhere, who really, really does not like bad boys. Much later, I discovered that old fella really, really dislikes lots of other folks as well. Gay people, for example, make it straight onto the bad-boy list, and on and on it goes, ad nauseam.

Young minds are impressionable. The once all-too-common notion—that if you got on the bad-boy side of the white-bearded fella's ledger, the best you could hope for is a fast train to Hell—can be hard to recover from. I've spoken to many former Catholics who feel that, in one form or another, the Catholicism of their youth was detrimental and even overtly harmful to their spiritual well-being. This is hardly surprising, given some of the stuff that was peddled back in the day. Certainly, ill-informed priests belting out this or that version of the hellfire and brimstone god of fear and trembling was less than helpful.

I do not want to detract from any conception of God that people hold dear. The punisher god, in various guises, certainly has a long history, with many adherents in multiple faith traditions. But for those of us who are among the seriously lost and broken—the people who have walked the long-suffering mile—the prospect of turning for comfort or spiritual help toward such a conception is decidedly unappealing. Or worse still, a source of more suffering.

In my case, this antiquated teaching about the god of fear came to an abrupt halt when I was twelve. To this day, I don't know exactly what happened. A new Irish priest had arrived in the parish. They were nearly all Irish in those days. Ireland had for a long time been a veritable priest factory. It seemed like there were gangs of them on every corner in the old country. From what my mother told me in hushed tones when I asked her about this incident a few years ago, certain whispers began circulating about the special interest this Roman-collared newcomer was taking in some of the small boys in the parish. When, a short time later, he dutifully arrived on our doorstep, there was a heated exchange between him and my father. He never came back, and that very night, all our ties with the church were immediately severed. Neither my parents nor my brothers ever returned to the church. The one exception to that rule would eventually be me.

These days, I leave the old punisher god to those who are more able or willing to accept such a concept. I walk instead with as much willingness as I can muster each day in complete solidarity with the wounded-healer God. The God who weeps when we weep, bleeds when we bleed, and gets down and dirty with really bad boys to pull them out of the mire. A God who calls to the heart with the beautiful words of the Desert Mothers and Fathers. Indeed, my walk is with the suffering servant of God[11] who held such appeal for Gandhi, Martin Luther King Jr., Bede Griffiths, and Francis of Assisi. But there were many rivers to cross and mountains to climb before I could claim to be even remotely in the same humble-hearted groove as any of these spiritual giants. For that to occur, I needed to encounter living "boats" and "helicopters" face to face, eyeball to eyeball.

---

11 Envisioned by the prophet Isaiah and later applied to life and death of the Galilean. See Chapters Fourteen and Sixteen.

Chapter Four

The Unforgotten Ones

I've heard it said that "God speaks through people," and I have found this to be true. Most folks who stumble onto the road less traveled, the humble-hearted way, the path to inner peace and freedom, have mighty exemplars from their past to draw upon with newly opened eyes. This fruitful pondering is helpful, not least because it reveals new lessons from past Wise Ones—boats and helicopters that were in the mix right from the get-go.

My father died suddenly and went to wherever indeed we go before I had my rude awakening and finally became ready. Today, I realize that he was one of my foundational teachers. He was, in many respects, an extraordinary man who, despite decidedly humble beginnings, ultimately built a successful forestry consultancy business in the UK. Stories about his encounters with English aristocrats abound in our family. Let's just say the conspicuous eccentricities of the bluebloods, which are legendary, paled against his Irish version of the same, which was always readily on display.

Among the many things I learned from him was that deference to another man, if deserved, is fine. But no man who expects such deference ever deserves it. Clothes and titles do not make the man, whether it is an Armani suit or the flowing robes of a power-dressing priest. Such symbols often enable the self-serving ego; the prideful self loves few things more than the control and deference of others.

Pride is a fearsome creature, something that everyone in search of a humble heart must eventually identify—not in others but within themselves. As the saying goes, "The real enemy is within." It is relatively easy to identify the prideful underpinnings of the ego in certain egomaniacs or in most institutional power structures. However, closer inspection will invariably reveal that this is just a mirror, a pale shadow of the real problem, which is my own prideful obsession with self. This is the game we are in; no one gets through this life unaffected by their own pride and the devastating results of its out-workings, especially a fella like me.

Socrates said, "The unexamined life is not worth living." But many go through life without even glimpsing internal pride, for pride has an uncanny ability to make itself invisible. I might be quite good at seeing yours, but regarding my own, I'm self-deluded to the max. Therefore, central to the spiritual journey, the quest for a humble heart, is the identification of the prideful ego, the pulling back of the cloak of self-deception. This task, however, is devilishly difficult because of the very nature of self-delusion. Indeed, it is an ongoing endeavor that I believe is simply not possible without the help of the One who is loving and compassionate. Self-centered pride is the number one block to an active relationship with the living God. But mercifully, in a Spirit-imbued world—if the biblical narrators are anything to go on—God gets an almighty kick out of saving fallen folks like me from this perpetual problem.

Most scripture scholars agree that the primary narrative in Hebrew and Christian scripture is about the God who saves.[12] The salvific One, whose capacity for giving another go to those who have seriously mucked up knows absolutely no limits. This is the God of steadfast love and mercy who breaks the chains of self-centered pride to free—even and perhaps especially—really, really bad boys. Today I don't have any doubt that every step taken in turning toward the living God is guided by that same ever-loving Spirit.

But I'm equally convinced that God works through people. The pursuit of a humble heart is always in the company of others. Looking back, I now realize that God was sending boats and helicopters to save me long before I could recognize them. Some were neither spiritual nor religious; at least, they wouldn't have seen themselves in those terms. Some were and are spiritual but not religious, a distinction that is important to them. Others comprise people who have spent a lifetime as members of religious orders.

Two people from my childhood occupy a special place in my heart. They were extraordinary teachers of what it means to be the very best that humans can be. They were very different from each other and from divergent backgrounds. One, a woman, my grandmother, was a devout, lifelong Irish Catholic. The other, an Englishman, was my best friend's

_____

12 This overarching biblical narrative, most frequently referred to by theologians as "salvation history," is further explained in Chapter Fifteen.

dad. He had no religious affiliation and probably had never heard of spirituality, much less seen himself as spiritual. Both showed extraordinary kindness to others.

My bestie and I had formed what would be a lifelong friendship in our early teens. We were both mad keen on horses; he had two, and I, of course, had none. My friend had a fine gray mare and his dad, taking an active interest in his youngest son's enthusiasm, purchased a ride-drive horse, a horse trained not only to be ridden but to pull a carriage as well. My friend would ride, and his dad would drive his horse-drawn carriage.

Then along comes Cormac! To say that I virtually lived at their home for the next two or three years is not an exaggeration. Neither is the fact that during that entire period, forgoing his own pleasure, my friend's dad actively encouraged me to think of his carriage horse as my own riding horse. Not only that, but my friend's family also treated me like I was one of their own—a status that continues to this very day. The generosity, the kindness, the active love these people showered on me was second to none.

Not long after I arrived in Australia in my early twenties, a letter arrived from my friend. As I read it, I could feel my heart breaking. His dad, my ideal man, had come home from work, sat down in his chair, and died. He wasn't the last person I wept from the heart over, but he was certainly the first.

I realize now that my mythologized version of him as the perfect man and teacher had its flaws. Even he, like all people, must have made the odd mistake in life. There is a danger in putting people on too high a pedestal because, if I've learned anything along the way, no one gets to be perfect. The expectation of perfection in others, and indeed myself, is but one of the prideful ego's great deceptions (more on that in Chapter Twelve). But boys need good male role models, and I had a truly great one. His example of selfless giving, of family-focused dedication, of how to be the real deal as a man, has stayed with me always. They just don't come any better than him. What a teacher.

In reality, I spent more time with my best friend's dad than I ever did with my grandmother. However, one of my brothers and I had an extended stay one summer with my grandparents in Ireland. Whatever perceptions I had developed about being poor, this was something else again. We stayed in the small house where my father and his twelve brothers and sisters had been born and raised, a house that was still receiving its water supply from a communal well shared with a cluster of other homes nearby.

I don't think that my grandparents for one moment ever considered themselves poor. This was no *Angela's Ashes* tale. The shadow of the great hunger, the famine of 1845–1849, still lingers in Ireland's rich culture. But poverty is relative. In their case, there was always handmade bread on the table; lots of potatoes, of course; bacon and cabbage together; and milk from cows that were hand-milked twice a day.

My grandfather was a fine and decent man, but boy could he blow! He had a volatility that I have rarely seen equaled, except in many of his own offspring, in whom the same trait is endemic. These are quintessential Irish people with all the associated passions. How thirteen of them grew up in that house with no one being murdered is possibly a minor miracle. But amid all this fire and fury was my grandmother, a veritable sea of calm. Perhaps it was the incredible contrast to most of those around her, but I don't believe I have ever seen anyone else quite like her. Maybe it was just her nature. Or perhaps at a certain point in her arduous life, she had seen the door marked Code of Peace, walked through it, and never looked back. For those who claim the Christ, the practice of radical inclusion is a definite requirement. She had mastered this and then some. Kindness and love exuded from her. That's who and how she was. What a teacher.

Some years later, my father and I were on a brief holiday in Ireland, more a pub crawl really. We stayed with my grandmother for two nights. By that time, my grandfather had gone to wherever indeed we go. That was not, however, anywhere near the extent of the grief that my grandmother had endured in the years just past. Those passions that I mentioned above had manifested in several of her children as Irish republicanism. As a result, one of my uncles had died two years earlier on a hunger strike in an English jail. I have never been in any doubt that my uncle's cause was a just one. But the suffering that comes with a death like his is beyond awful for those left behind. How would she be, I mused, as we drove up to the old house. She was as she had ever been—the same quiet dignity, the same intelligent simplicity, the same displays of overt kindness and love, the same humble heart! She was herself, and maybe even more so.

Before we departed, she quietly pulled me aside and did something that has stayed with me always. She reached out and held my face in her two gentle hands, and with all the tenderness that she personified, she said, "I've always had a special regard for you, Cormac." Even now, as I write this, over forty years later, I still feel the deep emotion that gentle touch and those few words of love evoked in me. What a teacher.

There is little doubt in my mind that she'd seen enough of me by then to know only too well that the fire and fury that is in my bloodline had passed to me in great measure. Did she perhaps have an inkling of the self-inflicted trouble that would eventuate from it?

Such passions are not always in error. They can, for example, be the drivers of the courage needed to seek justice and liberty. My truly courageous martyred uncle stands as a prime example of that. But when they become fueled by self-centeredness, pride, fear, and the like, as they were in me, things rarely end well. Past teachers, therefore, however extraordinary, were not enough to pull a fella like me back from the brink. New boats and helicopters would need to be sent. Sure enough, when I was finally ready, they appeared.

Chapter Five

Enter the Shaky-Handed Mystic

So, it came to pass a couple of months after my rude awakening while out walking early one cold Sunday morning that I stumbled upon a Catholic Church. I don't recall having any intention, prior to this moment in time, of retaking a pew. But as I passed by, I noticed one or two of the devout making their way into what I assumed must be an early morning Mass.

Surprised by the urge but less so by the misgivings that immediately followed it, I shuffled in behind them and plonked myself down at the back of the church. The surroundings were not unfamiliar. There were plenty of childhood memories to draw on. I had also, albeit briefly, dipped my toe back into the well a few years earlier. But those misdirected passions of mine had ensured I would soon fade away again.

This was an old-style church, with long rows of wooden pews separated by a central aisle that led up to a beautiful marble altar area. Above the altar, unsurprisingly, was an icon of the Galilean nailed to a cross. As I sat there looking up at him, perhaps for the first time, I felt some identification with the lonesome plight of this Jewish rebel from so long ago.

It immediately struck me that the attendance was miserably low. This was a large church, and there were maybe six or eight of us sitting there shivering in the cold. This differed from the memories of my youth when church services were invariably full. Then my hearing registered a *tap, tap, tap* and again a *tap, tap, tap*. As I glanced around to find the source, I realized it was the sound of a walking stick, which was barely supporting the most ancient priest I had ever encountered.

Fully clad in priestly gowns of the Roman variety, he was a tiny figure, hunched with age, making his way toward the altar. Tap, tap, tap. This was going to be a painfully slow procession. I wondered, by the look of him, whether someone would need to assist his faltering steps because I seriously doubted whether he'd make it to the altar unassisted. Then I noticed how his hands were shaking, not just the one that had a tenuous grip on the walking stick, but his free hand as well. Clearly, I thought, there is something seriously wrong with this old fella! Parkinson's disease, perhaps. *Tap, tap, tap*, and finally, after what seemed like an eternity, he got to the marble steps leading up to the altar. Will he make it up those steps, I wondered? Well, he did, but not without considerable difficulty.

Finally, he turned to face the few needy souls scattered far and wide in that enormous church, who were watching his mammoth effort to get to this point. He paused for a moment, attempting to straighten old bones that had not seen straight for decades. Now those shaking hands, palms exposed, were being spread as wide as their fragility would allow, and an enormous smile spread across his face, and he said, "Come on now, it's not that bad." At that very moment, I felt something perceptible move in my heart. What a teacher.

A few months passed, and I saw a notice somewhere about a gathering to discuss how to pray better. I kept thinking about it, and in the end, despite my usual misgivings, I went along. "What the hell!" I thought, "A fella like me can use all the help he can get."

I remember entering the room and realizing immediately that this was a huge mistake. It was one of those learned-type rooms, lots of books around the walls, and a long oval table with aging chairs arranged around it. But it wasn't the room that had set off alarm bells in my head, which were now screaming full bore, "Get the hell out of here!" It was the three women already seated at the table. I'd seen none of them before, but I knew exactly who and what they were. They were the extra holy ones, black-belt Catholic women. I'd seen legions of them in my childhood. The veil-wearing ones, who always did everything perfectly and seemed to keep a watchful eye on everyone else, including the priest, to help them be perfect too. They were the ones with the special job of confessing other people's sins as well as their own, if indeed they had any, because they were always first in line for confession and spent twice as long as everyone else in the confessional with the priest.

Oh, sweet Mother in Heaven, now I'm stuck in a room with three of the black belts. Could I escape? I felt like a caged animal. There was no way out! I mean, I was already in the room. I gingerly seated myself across from them. It might be okay, I thought; just keep your head down. It might not be too bad; you might make it out of here alive if you stay calm and say nothing.

At that moment, a door at the far end of the room opened, and a vaguely familiar sound reached my ears. *Tap, tap, tap; tap, tap, tap*, and sure enough, in shuffles my man, still as old as the hills, hunched, hands shaking involuntarily, supported by the stick. He makes his way to the table and sits down. Then there is that killer smile, and he says, "Welcome, everyone. I thought we might just go around the room, and everybody can say what their idea of God is." Oh no, not that! This is going to be all technical. My brain is racing now; is there still a way out? I knew I shouldn't have come. What did he say? "Just say what your idea of God is"? But I haven't got the foggiest clue of what my idea of God is. How would a fella like me know something like that? I knew I shouldn't have come.

However, the black belts are off and running now, smash, bang. The first one lays out a perfect doctrinal response. I glance at the priest. He'd have to be pretty pleased with that one, but he is expressionless. On to the second, bang, smash. She is more concise but no less brilliant, still nothing from the old fella. The third black belt then makes her play, easily matching and perhaps even outdoing the first two. I knew I shouldn't have come.

Then suddenly there is another player in the game. She's seated further down the table, and she must have been there all along, but I'm only now noticing her. I mean, she is next, and that means I'm not next. At least that's something. I notice she seems really young, maybe in her early twenties.

She's as pale as a ghost and thin as a wisp. She looks like someone who might know a thing or two about the dark places. All eyes are on her now because she's next. I'm not next. She pauses for what seems like a long time, her head goes down as if in thought, and then slowly rises again, and she says, "A whale."

My immediate and first thought after she said this is, "I think I love you!" But that's quickly supplanted by "That is definitely not the right answer to give to this ancient Jesuit priest." However, at that same moment and to my utter astonishment, the old guy is not just animated, he's up out of his seat, almost punching the air with one of his shaky hands and saying, "Yes, yes, yes. Now, we can really work with that." I do not know what I said when my turn came, or anything else that occurred at that meeting. Something had moved in my heart. What a teacher.

More months passed, and I read something about the spiritual exercises of St. Ignatius. He was a Spanish fella who, in the middle of the sixteenth century, came up with a practical program that people could follow if they wanted to have a more intimate relationship with God. It had something to do with meditation, what they called contemplative prayer. Apparently, it was this wacky mystic who eventually formed the Jesuits. He was another one of those out-there characters who have been emerging with regularity in every generation of Christians since the time of the Galilean. Seemingly, he coined the term "finding God in all things." I quite liked the sound of that, and I wondered if it might help explain why the old Jesuit with the shaking hands got so excited by the whale-God lady.

From what I could fathom, the Jesuits had been following the spiritual program set out by the Spanish mystic for hundreds of years. More recently, some of them had realized that Ignatius had intended his practical program of action for all God-seekers, not only the ordained and those in the religious life. After all, although the Spanish mystic would eventually become a priest, at the time he received the spiritual insights of his program, he certainly was not. He was living as a hermit in a cave outside of the city walls of Manresa, Spain.

Yes, I certainly liked the sound of this fella! I felt strangely drawn and comforted by the fact that he, like many other great mystics throughout history, had no formal theological training at the time of his mystical inspirations. Not infrequently, these folks were outliers from the cultural and religious norms of their time, but their authentic, lived embrace of age-old spiritual concepts like humility and love eventually makes them irresistible to those who seek the same.

This notice, however, was asking people to make an appointment to sit down and talk to someone, if interested. That sounded official. I mean, a fella could get locked into something that he really didn't want to do! No, I decided I'd give it a miss. However, I couldn't shake the idea of a program that helped people get up close and personal with God. What on Earth might that be about, I wondered? A more intimate relationship with the living God! Now, what's not to like about that? Perhaps I should ring the number. I mean, whoever they were, they couldn't make a man do anything he didn't want to do, could they? I mean, a fella like me, what did I have to lose? In my case, pretty much nothing, so eventually, I fronted up one morning to check the whole thing out.

CHAPTER SIX

ALL ABOUT THE "SPIRIT"

A short time later, I was sitting nervously in a room waiting for the low-down on this Ignatian spirituality thing. A door opened, and, yes, you guessed it: *tap, tap, tap*, in walked the diminutive and broken frame of the shaky-handed whale-God priest. "Well," said he, with that smile after we had quickly engaged in some general conversation, "would you feel comfortable telling me a little about yourself?"

I didn't feel comfortable about that at all. The god that I had learned about as a boy, the god of fear and trembling, who really doesn't like bad boys, was still deeply ingrained in me. How could I possibly tell my sorry tale to this man who was, you know, a priest, one of God's apparent watchmen on Earth! Or so I thought. But this was no ordinary priest; everything I had experienced of him up to that point told me that. It simply was not possible to be in his company and feel even the slightest bit of intimidation.

My tongue loosened, and I gave him the unabridged version of my life, all the time watching for the telltale signs of judgment that I was sure would appear. But none did. He had that rare talent of being a fully engaged listener—and something more, perhaps even rarer: he had complete empathy. This is something that I have since learned is usually only possible by someone who has known great suffering in their own life. By the time I finished, the beans had well and truly been spilled. I thought to myself, well, that should have put the kibosh on any chance of my progressing this thing. Right on cue, however, while this thought was forming in my mind, his head, which was bowed the whole time in what I thought might be some kind of meditative state, suddenly raised. "Excellent," says he. "I think you would be a perfect candidate for the spiritual exercises, and if you would allow me, I would like to guide you through them myself." Wow, I thought, me and the whale-God priest! I like the sound of that.

He then explained what I later realized were three imperatives. First, God has always had a deep desire to be in an intimate relationship of love with all of Creation, and the exercises are a way of entering more deeply into that intimacy. Second, there are "many ways," and the Ignatian path is but one of these. Third, committing fully to the process is vital, even if it makes no sense at all in the beginning. Spiritual wisdom comes from taking spiritual action. You've always got to walk the walk before you hear the talk. The only crucial requirement is to stay with it and complete the process. "Go home and ponder the proposal," he suggested. Ignatian folk, I was to discover, are all big on pondering! But I knew as we stood to say goodbye, and I shook his shaky hand that I was in. Even though I really still did not know what I was in for, or even why I wanted to be in.

If you had said to me a few years earlier that I would put my hand up for something like this, I would have thought you were crazy or laughed in your face. I mean a self-sufficient fella like me never imagined for a moment that I would fall so far or so hard. Much less that I'd be reaching for some strange meditation practice conjured up by a wacky mystic five hundred years earlier. However, such are the mysterious ways of the Spirit. The boats and helicopters that get sent to save us are rarely, if ever, what we could have foreseen or imagined. Indeed, just a few hours earlier, I didn't know that I was about to embark on the first phase of a radically inclusive spirituality of the heart, which opens wide the door to freedom. *For when the heart gets changed, everything changes.* As I now see it, I had always been on my way to this destination, right from the get-go, from my first-ever rebel breath.

I said at the start of this book that not everyone needs to be brought low, shaken and stirred, or reduced to a state of powerlessness and despair to begin the spiritual journey. But in my case, that is precisely what had to occur for me to become ready. It is only at that point of defeat that someone like me can become open to embracing a radically different way of living in this world. And it was no less than a completely fresh approach to life that was about to unfold before me.

None of this was happenstance or mere coincidence. Neither do I think it had much to do with what we normally consider rational thought. Let's face it: my track record in that department was dismally poor. I just seemed drawn toward this man, not so much by rational thought as intuition. I have since learned that, frequently, Spirit intuition is more in the realm of the heart than the mind. And without doubt, the external brokenness and the obvious empathy and compassion of this extraordinary priest had won me over completely, both heart and mind.

Little did I know, however, as we sat together again a few days later to make a start, that this mystic sitting opposite me was so highly regarded. Many believe he is one of the greatest teachers of the exercises ever. He was a man who, having already spent a lifetime as a Jesuit priest, in his mid-sixties became one of the chief proponents for giving the exercises to anyone and everyone who was willing. In the thirty years since—yep, that's right; turns out he was in his early nineties when he took me on—he had devoted himself entirely to just that.

As a man, I was in the minority among the multitude of women he had guided in this meditative practice to get up close and personal with the living God. Not only did he favor working with women, but many of these women had become influential teachers of the exercises in their own right. He told me one day, "Intuitively, women connect with the Spirit in their own hearts in ways that many men find difficult to achieve." Nor did he give a hoot whether the people who found their way to him were religious or not because he believed, with every fiber in him, that it was the living Spirit that enabled all these things to happen. He said of himself, "I'm just a conduit for the Spirit," and he carried these contemplative techniques to everyone from secular scientists to Buddhist nuns. What a teacher.

He was all about the Spirit, a Spirit that he believed had been active in the world from the year dot, long before the cultural phenomenon of widespread adherence to this or that organized religion ever occurred. Of course, he was a profoundly religious man, but he lamented that religiosity did not necessarily lead to an awareness of the absolute nearness of God. He said, "I sometimes feel that we in the West have lost touch with some of the best impulses of religion that are still practiced in the East, particularly the emphasis they place on the Spirit being active in the here and now, in everything." This is a very Ignatian view of things, which I suspect the founder of the Jesuits five hundred years earlier would have been entirely comfortable with.

I remember going to him one day with this question: "Should I be praying and meditating to God, Christ, or the Spirit?" I wanted to know. "Ah," says he, "that's easy. If you're talking and listening to one of them, then you're listening and taking to all three. Just let the Spirit guide you and remember we contemplatives allow the Spirit to speak to us through our imaginations, with hearts that are humbled by that same Spirit."

"Okay," said I, not grasping a word of what he had just said. "Do you mean, just sort of go with it?"

"That's it," said he. "Yeah, just go with it."

What a teacher.

As things turned out, I would be one of the last people to benefit directly from having him as a spiritual guide. Around the eighteen-month mark, just as I was completing the exercises, my little man, whom I had grown to love, suddenly became very ill and had to be housed in an aged-care facility. There he remained for the next few months before going wherever indeed we go. Unsurprisingly, there was plenty of weeping from the heart after his passing—and not just from me!

During those last few months of his life on Earth, I would drive past that facility at a particular time each Saturday morning. And who would I see every Saturday walking from the train station nearby to see the great mystic? None other than the thin-as-a-wisp, white-as-a-ghost, whale-God lady. Seems that I was not the only one to benefit from that meeting a couple of years earlier.

Looking back, he imparted many spiritual insights that were way beyond my comprehension during those early years. However, in the world of the Spirit, we are where we are and can only see what we can see and hear what we can hear at any given time. But among the crucial things that I came to realize more fully with the passing of time are the following:

- First, anyone willing to go lock, stock, and barrel on the meditation journey can discover the age-old wisdom of the mystics that the living Spirit dwells within our own hearts. Indeed, it is the source and essence that lives within all the beautiful variants of life on Earth.

- Second, at the very core of Ignatian spirituality and the foundation on which it sits is the pursuit of a humble heart. For it is only the humble-hearted who can embrace the intimate love that is on offer. This core principle of humility, in my experience, is so innate and important to pursuing any spiritual endeavor that it takes top ranking. This difficult-to-perceive and even more challenging-to-embrace essential spiritual practice is further explored in the subsequent chapters of this book.

- Third, "There are many ways." He had asserted this point at our first meeting, and the depth of this insight would become clearer as I progressed with him and other spiritual teachers over time. I will delve more deeply into the profound implications of this in Chapter Eight.

Fourth, the Ignatian meditation method employs the active use of each participant's imagination in what is called *imaginative prayer*. This somewhat rare and perhaps little understood way of meditating through the imaginative mind will be the focus of the next chapter.

CHAPTER SEVEN

IMAGINATIVE MEDITATION

Deploying the mind's innate and creative depths through the use of imagination is, I suspect, not what most people think of when they consider meditation. In my case, it was so far removed from any perceptions I had about what meditation might be that it was almost shocking when I was first introduced to it. I had thought meditation was, you know, all about somehow getting your mind completely still, devoid of any thought at all. This may well be the case for some meditation practices. But the wacky mystic Ignatius seems to have taken an entirely different view. In reality, I really didn't have the foggiest clue what meditation was. I'd heard the term, of course, although in the world that I occupied, I didn't know anyone who actually did it.

Except once, when I borrowed a meditation tape from a pal who told me in hushed tones that he was a meditator. Just lie down on your bed, he suggested, put the tape on, and follow what it says. Okay, I thought, even a fella like me could give that a whirl. Unfortunately, this little venture into the unknown was an unmitigated disaster. I followed the instructions dutifully enough, but once the tape started rolling, I was in trouble. The American lady was saying, "You are now feeling a distinct sensation in your toes."

"No, I'm not!" my incessant inner voice was saying. "I can't feel a thing."

"You can feel this sensation moving through your feet and ankles into your legs."

What? No, I can't!

"It's moving gently up through your body."

No, it isn't!

"You are feeling calm."

No, I'm bloody not! And now that I think of it, I don't even like the sound of your voice. Ah, to hell with this; I knew it wouldn't work! Game over. Arguing with the American lady on the tape who was attempting to lead me toward some form of meditative state, even I could realize, was probably not the intended outcome. But there you have it. That was the total of my meditation experience.

There was something else really odd for a Catholic of my generation about this Ignatian meditation stuff. I was being asked to enter deeply with my imagination into particular passages from scripture—yes, that's right, the actual Bible. Things are considerably different now, but I had grown up in a time when we of the Catholic persuasion left that kind of thing to the priests. They were the ones who read from scripture at Mass and then explained it to the rest of us.

Ignatius, however, had found himself literally banged up in an isolated castle in Spain after a cannonball had shattered one of his legs. The long period of recovery that followed changed his life. Left partially crippled and intensely bored, he began reading about the lives of the saints. And his fertile imagination went into overdrive. He discovered he could enter fully into the text as a participant, not just as a viewer. A full-on player in the adventures, not merely an onlooker.

Using imagination to enter deeply into the text would become the hallmark of Ignatian meditative practice. One could apply to scriptural texts the same creative flair one could bring to reading any other text. The unfettered imagination has to be unleashed on the narrative in order to grasp its many layers of meaning. Rather than silencing the mind, it's about allowing its creative energy and power to lead where it will. There is immense liberty and joy to be savored in such an endeavor because the spiritual insights that ultimately flow are plentiful.

I come from a culture where storytelling is a national pastime. It's not too difficult to see the central role that imagination plays in this, not just for the creators but for the listeners and readers too! However, the notion that this same use of the imaginative mind could apply to meditation was baffling to me. But meditation, of whatever kind, is just like anything else in life. If you want to get good at it, practice is the key, and you have to start somewhere, usually with one of those boat or helicopter teachers. After all, every great mystic began their journey on training wheels and then gradually over time, lots of time, got more proficient in the art.

From an Ignatian perspective, the contemplative endeavor need not be limited to scripture; it can apply to writing, poetry, film, artwork, nature, and so on. For novices like me, it was useful to consider the role that imagination has always played in these areas. Whose imagination hasn't been enlivened by some popular song, book, or movie? It is precisely in this same area of the mind where Ignatian meditation finds its roots and thrives. It is not about closing down one's thoughts but learning to suspend all the rational black-or-white, right-or-wrong stuff in favor of the imaginative, creative mind, even if it is only for a brief sojourn.

Entering this imaginative space in a book or a movie seems a lot easier than trying to do so when reading a passage of scripture. With the Bible, the go-to place in my mind is not imagination but what is right or wrong, correct or incorrect. It is helpful to remember, however, that these sacred texts mostly started their journey as stories told orally. Not as written texts that needed to be analytically understood, but as narratives, poetry, stories within a grand, overarching story, full of intrigue, myth, betrayal, loss, heroes who become rogues, and scoundrels who are made into heroes.

Of course, there is a vital place for detailed theological study, with all the crucial contextual analysis that it requires, but that's not the game we are in. This game does not require prior theological knowledge; in some respects, this can even be a barrier. Another obstacle is a literalist or fundamentalist way of reading scripture. Such an approach is an immediate showstopper to the imagination and is decidedly unhelpful to this venture. The only requirement is an ability to engage with the texts by entering into them with the imaginative mind. It is not incidental that biblical texts have in the past been a source of ongoing inspiration for poets, songwriters, novelists, artists, and moviemakers (and still are). These creative types are perhaps more easily able to engage the imagination and thus enter more deeply into the multiple layers of meaning that these texts convey.

But what about a fella like me whose default is to see the world through a black-or-white, wrong-or-right perspective? The answer, as already suggested, is practice. The creative impulse has to be exercised. I've just got to give it a red-hot go. It is also vital to affirm that this is a profoundly spiritual undertaking. The same Spirit that guides me to an attempt at meditation in the first place does not vacate the scene. In fact, the Spirit is the source of the text and the imagination that made it possible, and no less so an enabler of the eyes that view it. At no point is this a solitary adventure. It is rather a Spirit-imbued one. Mediating with the imagination fully liberated opens a needed window to allow that same Spirit to commune with us. This is a learned skill of engaging the mystic mind, the imaginative mind, the mind infused by the Spirit.

You may think that this is all the exclusive stuff of the mystically inclined, but experience has shown me it is available to all. There are, without doubt, many ways, but every one of them requires consistent and sustained practice to come to fruition. Quick fixes do not exist in the meditation game. However, from an Ignatian spirituality perspective, all that's needed is a willingness to make a start, an embrace of the imagination, and a commitment to stick with it; the Spirit takes care of the rest.

While entering the imaginative mind is one way the Spirit can commune directly with every one of us, going it alone in this venture is fraught with danger. These flights of fancy into the imagination frequently turn out to be just that: fanciful imagination! Therefore, it is always necessary to bring the resultant pondering, usually written, back to planet Earth for careful discernment. This discernment process will always require honestly sharing with someone else, usually a spiritual guide, whatever wacky thoughts seem to emerge. She or he will be indispensable here because their long experience will undoubtedly include having a whole truckload of wacky thoughts themselves. They will have discovered that what at first might seem a very noble undertaking, some grand urging of the Spirit, regularly turns out to be the prideful ego all dressed up as virtue, leading in precisely the wrong direction.

In my experience, Ignatian meditation rarely results in a call to make immediate world-shattering changes in the way we are already living. Rather, the call is to make incremental changes that make that way of living more Spirit-aware, imaginative, and purposeful. I might feel that I am being called to scurry off to a cave somewhere with my loincloth and very little else. But on closer examination, it may turn out I've just got to listen more to others, give the bus driver a thank you every day, pay closer attention to those flowers in the garden, and pray and contemplate without ceasing. A mystic must learn that careful pondering, discernment with others, and time are crucial before major life changes ensue.

Neither is it necessarily the case that mystics, we folks who meditate, have to abandon all worldly possessions, although it may be for some. I learned a great lesson in this from my number one go-to guy, the humble, wealthy one mentioned in previous chapters. Although his spiritual practice is not the Ignatian one, it is in every respect just as vibrant.

I remember him telling me that when many years ago he first started on the spiritual path, he made several very costly business decisions, thinking that was what his new outlook required—you know, now that he was all spiritual. Later, with the help of others, he could see that this was foolishness, pride in reverse, masquerading as spirituality.

There is nothing inconsistent about pursuing business ethically while listening to the urgings of the Spirit. I am informed enough about my rich go-to guy's activities, none of which are ever trumpeted by him, to know that his wealth (which may well have tripled during the time I have known him) has, along the way, benefited many people. Had he not been able to generate this wealth, these folks would otherwise not have received that help. Now, that's real-time spirituality in action.

Ultimately, meditating through the use of the imagination, to enter deeply into scriptural texts and thus the realm of the Spirit, will be counterintuitive for many folks—especially people who follow other meditation practices that seek to quieten the mind more fully. Again, deploying the imaginative mind to meditate is just one of many ways. However, the freedom to embrace our innate imagination makes this method easily accessible. Anyone who has an imagination—and that means everyone—can give this thing a go, even a fella like me.

Ignatian meditation also has a venerable pedigree of nearly five hundred years of practice, from which has emerged profound new insights regarding perhaps the greatest story ever told. I mean the story about the God who walks in lockstep, heart to heart, breath for breath with everyone and everything in what one of my later spiritual guides called "this beautiful but broken world." Imagine that! Make no mistake, when this form of meditation gets a persistent trial, it is an absolute game-changer in how we see the world.

CHAPTER EIGHT

THE UNITY-IN-DIVERSITY THING

Tender mercies certainly flow to people who give meditation, in whatever form, a consistent try. It is an indispensable tool in the spiritual transformation of the heart. Among these mercies must surely be a new appreciation of the immense diversity that God has created in the world. This is like life-giving rain on what had been barren land. Suddenly blind eyes can see, and hard hearts beat to a shiny, new drum. On my trek, I gradually realized that a full embrace of diversity is very much part of the journey. Indeed, I was to learn that the "many ways" have a far wider application than just the multitude of different approaches to meditation.

A pride-fueled rejection of diversity has always plagued religious and secular movements. This elitist approach is entirely unhelpful, and the terrible consequences, both personal and collective, that flow from such blinkered views, abound in history. The blind-eyed, self-deceived pride that I alluded to in Chapter Four is the primary culprit here. Nobody entirely escapes the self-deluding juggernaut of pride and its "us or them," "who's in and who's out" dehumanizing results. Our ability to self-deceive knows no bounds. It is a sad reality that this pernicious trait is just as common among religious folk as anyone else. However, in the religious setting, it is especially insidious because it hides behind lofty ideals.

Not so in the sacred space, the here-and-now, up-close-and-personal-with-the-living-God place. In that space, diversity in all things is an unending, Spirit-infused phenomenon of immense and ever-changing beauty, to be ever more deeply embraced with the awe that perhaps only the humble-hearted of any practice or faith can fully muster. Put simply, diversity is in all that God creates and inhabits.

There is, of course, unity in all and between all things, and this is the wonderment of a world, a universe, or multiverse imbued with the God who is love and compassion. The great mystics, from whatever time or tradition, all eventually arrive at this same conclusion. They know that God and love are inseparable, the same. Indeed, it is this love that is the creative source and glue that binds life together in all its diverse and beautiful variants.[13] As it is written, "We are many parts, but we are all one body" (1 Cor 12:12). Unity is never at the expense of diversity. Rather, the embrace of diversity enhances unity.

After the passing on of my much-loved shaky-handed mystic to wherever indeed we go, I was to discover just how far diversity (the many ways) extends. By that time, I was well and truly ensconced in the church where I had first encountered him. What had begun as attendance at Sunday Mass morphed into my showing up daily. I soon realized that

---

13 This key principle is further explained in Chapter Seventeen.

my guy was certainly not the only Jesuit priest living in the house opposite the church. A whole gang of old Jesuits lived there, two of whom would become future spiritual guides to me. I look back now at the treasure trove that these men proved to be. It was an amazing time.

What was striking about this group was its diversity! They were all Jesuits, but with equal vigor as different from each other as chalk and cheese. It is no exaggeration to say that you could have lined them up, side-by-side, given them the same biblical text, and six entirely different and even conflicting takes would emerge. They were reading from the same song sheet, but what came out would do justice to an orchestra. My belief that there was a wrong or right interpretation of these things was blown seriously out of the water.

I remember one of them saying to me one day, "The Spirit doesn't allow us to be perfect, but makes us perfectly unique so we can practice perfecting unity with one another through love." That is as good a description of unity in diversity as any I have encountered. And yes, he was a philosopher. Funny the things you remember!

As the scales fell from my eyes, I began to notice yet more examples of diversity within that little Catholic Church community. By this time, I had also become a kind of unofficial trainee under one of what I call the Quasimodo folk. These are the frequently slightly odd-looking, nearly always well-aged, often shadowy figures that you can usually see scurrying about in the background in most Catholic churches before things get underway. Some of these Quasimodos are truly amazing people. You might think at first sight that you are witnessing some poor old decrepit soul, committed for who knows how many years to menial tasks, when you might just be looking at the real thing, God with skin on! Busy practicing the main game of active humility through other-centered love in action. Getting to hang out with some of these selfless servants can be transformative, if for no other reason than to learn that perceptions are frequently wrong.

One of these Quasimodos that I eventually came to know well has got the full tool kit in place as far as looks go. She is as old as the hills, and has the *tap, tap, tap* thing happening, not to mention a hunched back. No one, including herself, can quite remember how long she has been around the church—multiple decades, at least. Like most of the other Quasimodos I've encountered, she had taken the journey and well and truly arrived at the humble-hearted place. They are among the great mystics of our time, who crave neither podium nor recognition, which is fortunate because, sadly, they rarely get much of either. This woman had long since retired from her professorship at a leading university. Like I said, looks can be deceiving. At any given Mass—and the Quasimodos are at most of them—she might just be the smartest person in the room, but you would never know it.

Clearly, these folk represent a very select group of people, and not too many even committed Catholics desire to enter their humble realm. You would expect, therefore, that while as a group they represent one of the many ways, they would at least among themselves be on the same page in terms of their beliefs. To some extent, this is true; they are people who have become ever more deeply engaged by the Spirit in the enduring and immense mystical beauty of the Mass ritual. My interactions with them, however, have shown me that for all the unity of the Mass, how the Spirit moves each one of them is unique. Turns out that diversity is as rampant among these folks as it is among the diverse people with whom they share the Mass, both in the pews and on the altar.

Certainly, the Mass, with its long tradition and global participation, maintains continuity. Few other things one can take part in have a two-thousand-year tradition. For Catholics past and present, the Mass is an intentionally unifying experience. It was ever thus. It is because of its tried and tested power to draw diverse people together as one through a transformative relationship with God that it has been so vigorously maintained. There is a participatory harmony about the whole ritual, guided by strict rules that keep the show on track. In a diverse Catholic setting, it is usually the black belts, ordained and not, who seem to occupy the space of maintaining the guide rails that preserve unity for most, while simultaneously trying to keep the mystics from drifting too far out to sea.

Structural rules, though, however necessary, are not the main game. It is important to remember that the Crucified One was a serial rule-breaker, disregarding anything that ran counter to his core teaching of other-centered inclusive love. The Mass is an ancient tradition that depends on the active participation of the Spirit. Without it, the desired unity descends into a dubious set of human-imposed rules.

Once the Spirit gets into the game, diversity is an endemic reality because it now reflects the creative impulse of the One who is loving and compassionate. Finding unity within such a vast plurality is one of the great and mysterious gifts received on the path to freedom. For in the end, the unity in diversity that unequivocally binds all as one is the selfsame love that is God. It may well be that it is only in the humble-hearted place, the unified-with-the-Spirit space, that such unity in diversity can be perceived with ease. There are indeed many ways, but they coalesce through the prism of radically inclusive love.

CHAPTER NINE

MORE BOATS AND HELICOPTERS REQUIRED

I am a product of practical spiritual experience gained over an extended period by walking the talk of spiritual practice. This is decidedly ordinary, not otherworldly, and comes from the trials and tribulations of everyday life that we all experience, not from highfalutin, esoteric spiritual theory. Hanging out with folks who demonstrably exude diversity was thus the window into realizing its absolute pervasiveness in all that God creates.

There was a time when I hoped for an almighty, once-and-for-all, done-and-dusted spiritual experience. You know, the choirs of angels, straight to the mountaintop, job-done thing. I know people who have undergone dramatic spiritual changes like this, but I'm not one of them. I am what some of my sober boozehound friends call "a slow learner and quick forgetter." A fella who has needed not one but a series of boats and helicopters to guide my faltering steps.

I'm not sure how I came under the guidance of Jesuit spiritual guide number two. I don't recall asking him. It just kind of happened after we had a chat one day about where I was up to in the spiritual exercises. I laid out my spiel about imaginative prayer and how I was giving it a red-hot go. Then I confidently added that I might not be a meditation master yet, but hey, I've got this thing.

The long silence that followed seemed, with every second that passed, to open a huge drain down which my confidence was rapidly disappearing. Eventually, he spoke: "There is so much more to the exercises than the rudimentary understanding that you seem to have gained." What? Rudimentary! I thought. But I'm eighteen months in. I mean, a fella like me, surely rudimentary is not where I'm at after all this time? I'm crestfallen and dumbstruck now. So, he continues: "Yes. The two of us should go right back to the beginning and do the whole thing again." What, right back to the beginning! A fella like me? But what about all the progress I've made? I'm thinking. He persists: "You don't seem to have grasped the fundamentals, especially regarding repetition, humility, and the vital importance of the awareness examen."

I had to concede, albeit with a good deal of reluctance, that the humility thing, whatever that was, had slipped past me. And regarding "repetition" and the "awareness examen," I was at a complete loss because I could recall nothing at all about either of these practices.

Many years later, I would learn that my guy number two was seriously out on a limb in the Ignatian-guide world regarding his application of "repetition." Most Ignatian mystics apply this crucial meditation tool as a method of repeating or staying with the same passage of scripture over a number of days. For him, though, this had developed into a license to have his retreatants *repeating all of the exercises* in an endless cycle. I've since seen the eyes of more than a few experienced Ignatian folk raised to Heaven regarding this approach. But that was his schtick. He was the rebel repetition man, and I had now fallen under his care.

So away we went, repetition after repetition, repeating all the exercises, or as he called it, "going deeper." On and on, around and around we went ad infinitum for several years. I now realize that the Spirit never falters in the helicopters and boats that get sent our way. In retrospect this laborious repeat-and-go-deeper process served me well because my ongoing struggle with depression had played havoc with my ability to absorb and hold information, spiritual or otherwise. Though had I an inkling at the time that working through the exercises, only to repeat the whole thing again, was not the norm, I'm sure I would have thrown in the towel.

Not only that, but our relationship, which ultimately extended for almost a decade, was sometimes fraught. The repetition rebel had a way of challenging me that I never enjoyed. Nor was my discomfort limited to the repeat-and-go-deeper process. You don't spend as much time with someone as I did with him without their views on a variety of subjects becoming apparent. We clashed frequently over what I felt were his misogynistic and racist views. Saying that we clashed, however, is not an apt description. It was more that I objected strongly with those old passions of mine, and he was entirely unconcerned whether I agreed with him or not. Looking back, it was like real-time training in diversity. Diversity only gets real when you are confronted with views completely opposed to your own. (More on that in a later chapter.)

Mercifully, by this time, he had introduced what turned out to be a game-changer in my spiritual development, the aforementioned practice known as an awareness examen or examination of conscience. Essentially, it is a twice-a-day review of the hours just past. This enables development of the awareness that there are two things at play in whatever is going down in my little world: one is the ever-present Spirit in all things; the other is the pervasiveness of the self-seeking ego. Awareness of the presence of the living God is where all the good fruit in life surely hangs. However, there must also be, parallel to this, a constant awareness of the ego-self and how often it is from this fruitless place that so much of my thinking and actions emanate. This short, twice-daily meditation, together with the main meditation period each morning, is where the rubber really hits the road. *The spiritual life is not a theory; it is a practice. It's a doing thing, not a thinking thing!*

My repetition rebel told me that Ignatius himself valued the Spirit-invoked practice of "awareness above all else." It is truly a mighty thing because, over time, with persistent practice, one can indeed get drawn ever more often to the good fruit and less frequently to the fruitless. In my case, genuine progress in the radically inclusive, absolute game-changing spirituality of the heart emerged when the practice of this spiritual tool became grooved into my life. This alone would have been an invaluable gift! But I learned so much more from this man along the mystic way before eventually he too went wherever indeed we go. What a teacher.

For all their many differences in how they practiced Ignatian meditation, my first two spiritual guides had one thing in common—an emphasis on humility. Here lies the limitless treasure at the core of this spiritual practice: the ability to embrace the other, warts and all, depends on a deeper embrace of humility not just as a concept but as a way of being.

Now, I've heard it said, "There are no coincidences; there are only God-instances." It is therefore not surprising that my next guide was pretty much humility on legs. I had long admired him, particularly because, so far as I could see, he truly dwelled in the humble-hearted place. I knew, for example, that he was a published scholar of scripture. But his innate humility enabled him to come down from the heights of academia and provide spiritual insights and teaching that were experiential and tailored for all.

As we began our walk together, it was soon clear that, for him, it was all about the heart. He told me, "It is perfectly possible to perceive God with the mind, but the mystic knows such perceptions are just a way station, on the way to where all the action really is, and that is in the heart." Not that he would deprecate the mind. He was a Jesuit, and they, almost without exception, are mad keen on educating minds.

His journey was decidedly different from my first two teachers. Following his regular education, he spent fifteen years of his young life becoming a Jesuit and shortly thereafter became a missionary in India. There he would stay for nearly fifty years before returning to Australia as an old man. He explained that there were two really important things that he learned in India. First, he had gone there expecting to bring the one true faith to the poor heathens, but what he discovered was that God had been among these people long before Christianity ever became a thing. Second, he said, "I spent my first fifteen years as a missionary in India unlearning everything previously learned so I could become a true contemplative mystic."

He never faltered in his commitment to the Christian faith. However, he became increasingly convinced that his own religious practice could learn much from the culture in which he had become immersed. Along the way, he joined the dots between the Hindu virtue of humility and what he came to believe was also the core of the Christian message— that, ultimately, the pursuit of a humble heart was the main game! *For when the heart gets changed, everything changes.* This was the spiritual imperative above all else. But he was equally adamant that it was a doing thing, an active-practice thing, right in the middle of what he called "this beautiful but broken world."

This is one of the many paradoxes of the spiritual life. Practical action in everyday life in order to pursue the goal is vital. However, a humble heart is not in any way something we achieve; it is always entirely a gift of the Spirit. I realize that this may sound like a bunch of gobbledygook, but as the wise guides tell us, you've got to actually do this stuff before it makes any sense. Making sense of it before you are on the journey is highly unlikely.

We are dealing here with the mysterious way that God whispers to the heart. Yep, it turns out that God is the great heart-whisperer. Hearing and acting upon these gentle whispers must become a primary purpose in the quest for freedom. This is what Ignatian mystics call discernment, for it is only in the humbled heart, devoid of the mind's ego distractions, that God's gentle whispers become loud and clear. Now, some folks find this listening-heart space quickly, but it took me several years of practice and plenty of missteps before I even realized that attempting to listen to God with the heart was, in fact, the goal. We are where we are and can only hear what we can hear and see what we can see at each juncture in this unfolding, lifelong journey. It's really a matter of, you know, just going with it.

I also discovered during the next few years with guide number three that there was nothing airy-fairy or otherworldly about this humble-hearted endeavor. Certainly, mystics go to the mountain to listen to God's whispers, but then they come back down and get busy doing stuff, God stuff, other-centered, radically inclusive love stuff. Discerning what the Spirit urges in the heart is the ultimate destination of the quest, but it always leads to practical action.

Mr. Humility on legs was as much a mystic as anyone I have ever met. However, he helped convince me that if my relationship with God did not translate into humble-hearted, other-centered love on the ground, it would be just smoke in the wind. If I'm getting a hotline in the heart with God, you can bet your boots that the marching orders will always be the same. Get out there and get down and dirty with that same Spirit in this beautiful but broken world. Humility is always a doing thing. What a teacher!

CHAPTER TEN

KEEPING IT REAL

A true litmus test for entering the humble-hearted space is whether we can put into action the whispers of the Spirit received in the heart. Keeping it real, however, will probably include many missteps—faltering regularly is part of the deal.

Let me address two misconceptions about humility. One is the delusion that we can become so God-centered, so plugged into the heart hotline with the Divine, that human advice is no longer required. The other, which is common, is equating humility with humiliation.

Regarding the first, my difficulty is that I always want to present as if I already know the answer to any situation—as if I am the hearer-of-God-whispers supreme. Or failing that, simply wise to the ways of the world. My pride deceptively resists revealing myself to others as vulnerable and unknowing. Yet, vulnerability is a key indicator of living humbly. Self-sufficiency is never an ally of the humble way but one of its chief obstacles. It is pride writ large.

Imagining oneself to be so fully Spirit-aware that mere mortal advice is superfluous can be a dangerous phase of the spiritual journey. This may be true for some rare individuals, but for a fella like me, such an attitude is one more bastion of self-deceived pride that needs to be surrendered constantly. Crucially, this surrender always involves others. It is the verdict of the ages that honestly sharing with another, revealing yourself as unknowing, vulnerable, and frequently off track, will do more to take you to the humble place than just about anything else. As discussed earlier in relation to "imaginative meditation," going it alone in spiritual matters is seldom wise and not infrequently disastrous. The humble-hearted way always includes discernment with others who know all about being self-deceived in this beautiful but broken world and bear the scars of their own misdeeds to prove it. We don't need Roman-collared people for this vital process, although I don't rule them out. We do need someone who knows the way because they've walked it.

Realistically, though, the traps of prideful ego are an unavoidable part of the journey. Indeed, on the path to inner peace with purpose, it is the many falls that provide the impetus for ongoing spiritual growth. Seen in this light, the falls ought to be celebrated; from them, we learn so much. I learned that punishing myself for making what will inevitably be a lot of missteps is debilitating and not helpful at all.

I recall the humble one saying to me one day when I had mucked up badly and was subsequently giving myself an unholy lashing, "Jump down off the cross, Cormac; we might just need the wood." The living God who is loving and compassionate is never into the punishing game, so why do it to yourself? For, as surely as the beauty of God dwells deep within each one of us, so too does the brokenness. Falls must come; they are inevitable. It's just part of being human.

As stated above, humility never means being humiliated. A little theology is helpful here. From a Catholic perspective, the whole person—body, mind, and spirit—is a creation and dwelling place of God. This is a first principle known as "the inherent dignity of the human person," which also finds secular expression in the Universal Declaration of Human Rights.[14]

In biblical terms, each one of us is created in the image of God—what theologians call "Imago Dei."[15] This confers a special dignity on humanity but also, by implication, a responsibility regarding how we view and behave toward the other, every other. In the Creation story—found in the Book of Genesis—we are all effectively depicted as God with skin on (Gen 1:26–27). Therefore, this same section of the Bible (Gen 18:1–8) emphasizes the welcoming of strangers. The Hebrews later codified this important prerogative of welcoming the outsider in the hospitality code (Lev 19:33–34; Exod 23:9). Nor do you have to wait long in the biblical narrative before you confront the issue of unity in diversity. In fact, the Creation story is a case in point, for there are two creation stories; the alternate version is where we encounter Adam and Eve and the famous narration about the fall of man (Gen 3:1–24).

Like all scripture, these texts are subject to wide interpretation. My third spiritual guide, being no slouch

---

14 UN General Assembly, *Universal Declaration of Human Rights, 2*17 (III) A (Paris, 1948).

15 The concept of Imago Dei is further explored in Chapter Thirteen.

in biblical scholarship, developed his oft-repeated dictum about "this beautiful but broken world" by combining both creation stories. Thus, the beautiful is all that God creates, including humanity, in God's image, while the broken is our mythic fall—the result of egocentric behavior, driven by self-centeredness, self-deception, fear, pride, and their various combinations.

The critical point is that individually or collectively humiliating another person violates their innate dignity as a creation of God. There are no circumstances where this fundamental principle does not apply—whether it is toward someone I think deserves a shot of ego-deflation or the humiliation of one group by another. It is important to understand that humiliation or degradation of others never emanates from the God-given dignity, the beauty, within perpetrators. Therefore, there is nothing humble-hearted about passively accepting such behavior from a person or collective.

Mahatma Gandhi is a prime example. Here was a man few could doubt was living the humble-hearted way. However, he could not accept the humiliation and degradation of the Indian people from a foreign imperialist power. His nonviolent campaign for Indian independence is proof positive that the humble-hearted, in all their innate dignity, should never accept humiliation. Rather, the spiritual call is to oppose such humiliation nonviolently. Many have done so throughout history—not the least of whom was the Galilean Hasid, who influenced Gandhi's approach.

Again, humility never means being humiliated; the humble-hearted mystic must keep it real. If my own innate dignity or the dignity of those around me is being violated, it will without exception be from one or more perpetrators who are acting from the broken, selfish, proud place within themselves, and this cannot stand.

The implications here are stark: it will always be insufficient if I limit my concern to whether I am the subject of humiliation. In order to grow in my innate dignity, I must be equally concerned and just as proactive in protecting the innate dignity of others. Whenever and wherever humiliation and degradation of others occurs, the innate dignity of everyone is trampled underfoot and diminished. It is not incidental that the humble-hearted exemplars just mentioned, and many like them across all times and cultures, had the innate dignity of others as their primary motivation for action.

Certainly, compassion needs to flow in all situations where humiliation is being perpetrated because we are dealing with spiritual disease or brokenness. We live in a beautiful but broken world, and few indeed get through this life without being both victims and perpetrators of humiliation. I may think, for example, that I rarely, if ever, impose such harm on the God-given dignity of those I come into contact with. However, my scorecard might not look as good if I consider the degradation of millions of people around the world every day. Where anyone is humiliated, all suffer the loss of dignity. This includes victims, perpetrators, and all of us who blind ourselves to suffering and are the direct or indirect beneficiaries of it.

The temptation of my own prideful brokenness is to enter the blame game, to point the finger at others and exonerate myself. This can lead me to do nothing other than complain about the sad state of the world. Or worse, it may set me off on a self-righteous, ego-driven crusade, punishing others who are fellow sufferers of spiritual illness.

It is imperative, therefore, to seek the humble-hearted place where the living God, who is the manifestation of pure love and compassion, combines with my inherent humanity to plan practical action that heals and counters humiliation. To respond to the broken world, we need to be immersed in its beauty! And for a fella like me, only a humble-hearted space can provide that perspective. It is only from that space, the God-within place, that the needed compassion can flow.

Keeping it real, however, requires acknowledging this is just one of many ways. The central pillar of the ethics of the secular Universal Declaration of Human Rights is the inherent dignity of the human person. In this beautiful but broken world, it is frequently the case that secular human-rights activists from every corner of the world are more embedded in the beauty than many a fella like me who bangs on ad nauseam about humble hearts and spirituality. These folks are out there keeping it real. All too often, they are advocating for people whose dignity is being plundered in the here and now by religionists of every stripe. Now, there's a humble thought for my heart to ponder! There is plenty of brokenness to go around, and clearly it is not only religious people who perpetrate humiliation. But whatever its source, accepting it in any form as a precursor of humility is mistaken because it certainly is not.

CHAPTER ELEVEN

THE WISE ONES

I have said much about the mystic men sent to save me. But they're not the only boats and helicopters that have kept me from drowning. There have also been female teachers on the journey. I call them the "Wise Ones." Many of them have more humility in their little finger than a fella like me ever will, even if I were to live three lifetimes.

These women are the great carriers of heart wisdom, who seem intrinsically attuned to the gentle urgings of the Whisperer—folks who, in my experience, are born into that role rather than made. When it comes to knowing innately important truths about this beautiful yet broken world, they are the gold medalists! As storms gather and come lashing through our lives, they are voices of reason, soothing ruffled feathers and healing broken wings. I don't know why they are nearly always women. That seems to be the way of things—invariably, they are in the trenches, carrying the load. I have yet to meet a Wise One who hasn't known great personal suffering—suffering that, in them, is mysteriously transformed into other-centered love.

The Wise Ones are the walking, talking, compassion-doers of the world. Perhaps that's why we broken people get drawn to them like bees to honey. I've seen them doing their compassion thing in far-flung places, way out on the margin's edge, tending to the walking wounded. Empathy is their trademark. It keeps them mostly away from the lofty, on-high places, preferring instead to seek out and grasp the trembling hands of troubled hearts on the boulevard of broken dreams—a place where many of us, one way or another, take a reluctant stroll.

I am both baffled and intrigued by their overtly humble ways. I mean, how could I not be, given that almost everything I have been trying to do for years finds its fulfillment in deeper humility. Yet, when you get up close and personal with the Wise Ones, you see that they have lashings of it—effortlessly—as if the sprinkling of the Divine among us is double-dosed in their case. They are naturally humble; you won't find a smidgen of hubris among them.

Many of the Wise Ones I've encountered are spiritual rather than religious. Most religions have the unfortunate and dubious habit of entrenching male hierarchy and control, not to mention an insistence on often-moribund rules that are upheld ruinously for many. None of this is even remotely conducive to the space where humble hearts can flourish. Small wonder that so many of the Wise Ones don't bother themselves much with organized religion. I strongly suspect that their kind has never easily found a home where black-belt rule-makers are in the ascendency. It's easy to imagine—indeed, I would bet—that among the many women cruelly burned at the stake as heretics and witches during the Middle Ages, there were more than a few Wise Ones.

So, who are they? My grandmother, whose humility I wrote about in Chapter Four, was one. The professor Quasimodo mentioned in Chapter Eight is another. My mother-in-law, who has now also gone wherever indeed we go, was yet another. She was quite a lady; her capacity to see the beauty in all things and lay aside the brokenness was amazing. I know this because I am a direct beneficiary of it. Even many years after her only daughter and I divorced and having experienced so much of me at my destructive and raving worst, she would light up like a ray of sunshine whenever I visited her during her many stays in hospital, announcing with great joy to any nurse or doctor present, "This is Cormac, my Irish son-in-law!" When you're held in the embrace of one like her, you're held for all time. What a teacher.

As fate would have it, I was with her when she took her last breath, and yes, I wept from the heart. Not that she would have seen it in those terms. She had told me two weeks prior, "I'll soon be going for a long sleep." Her spirituality was such that she believed her current earthly life was but one of multiple lives she had experienced before. I recall being confounded many years ago while standing with her in the ruins of an old Irish castle. She suddenly exclaimed, as if it were a common occurrence, that she had stood within that same castle centuries earlier. Reincarnation does not form part of any Christian doctrine that I am aware of, but that didn't hinder her in the slightest from holding such beliefs. Simultaneously, she could turn on a sixpence and tell me about the chats she regularly had with Jesus. Indeed, she seemed more intimately attuned to the ways of the Galilean than many who claim him.

That's one of the remarkable things I've noticed about the Wise Ones. Most have an amalgam of beliefs, a kind of spiritual soup, always brewing, to which they are constantly adding the finest ingredients. Among the Wise Ones, this amalgamation is a thing of profound beauty. It is as normal and inherent in them as their humble compassion. It is a tragedy that folks like these are often hounded out of religious communities, and my mother-in-law was no exception. Several Christian churches showed her the door, fools that they were. She may have been one of the most Spirit-imbued people who ever walked among them.

Another of these Wise Ones, although she wouldn't see herself that way—they never do—is a dear friend I've known for nearly fifty years. She's got the full package of the humble-hearted, wise-one thing happening. Super smart, she's had a stellar career as a mother, business consultant, and stalwart of her community. She just exudes the humility that translates into active compassion for others. And yes, she too has well and truly known the suffering place! I have long admired her capacity for kindness, which now also extends to being the co-founder with her husband (my previously mentioned oldest friend) of a charity in Africa. She seems entirely accepting of the brokenness of others, which she comforts with her own intrinsic beauty. The special gift of being open to all forms of spirituality without being captured by any applies to her in great measure.

I recall banging on one day about the problem of male hierarchy in the Catholic Church and proposing that we should put the female Wise Ones in charge. She listened to this for a while and then simply said, "Who says they would want to be in charge?" What she didn't say, but I later realized, was that my argument was fatally flawed—my male-feminist credentials were fallacious, and my bleeding heart was self-deceived patriarchy. I told you she was smart!

On another occasion, I jumped up on my high horse and used a snappy slogan I'd picked up or made up (I'm not sure which). "There is no Me without the We," I declared with more than a little triumphalism. This mantra, I argued, epitomized the ethics that should apply in the Western world because we had descended into a cult of individualism. This "Me" focus, I contended, would not end well unless there was a complete reversal of this trend and the adoption of the common good, of egalitarianism, as the supreme ethic.

I had thought she would be on board with this little rant, but I was wrong. With her normal grace, she matched my slogan with one of her own. "Neither," said she, "can there ever be a We without the Me." Then she laid out her ethical position: unless individual liberty has primacy, the utopian We vision that I was advocating would fail. In fact, if history is our guide, then such utopias usually descend rapidly into stifling creativity, entrenching demagoguery, and crushing people's innate dignity. I told you she was smart! This was one of those conversations that stay with you. After much pondering, I eventually realized that both propositions were equally true! "There is no Me without the We, and there is no We without the Me." There is a balance that needs to be found in all things. One of the great virtues of the Wise Ones is their ability to gently guide others toward balance. Because it is precisely in the center where all the genuine beauty of enduring truth occurs. What a teacher.

Yet another Wise One worthy of mention is an Irish nun I encountered some years ago. A remarkable woman, then in her eighties, she had been traveling the world for several years giving talks about spirituality. There was nothing ordinary about this old nun because she was a self-confessed recovering alcoholic. Yep, an Irish alcoholic nun! I thought, I've got to hear this; She sounds like my kind of girl.

The candor with which she spoke about her journey was remarkable, but she also possessed that great Irish gift of the gab. A natural storyteller, she could use humor with ease and captivate her gatherings for hours. If humility had not been innate in her during her booze-soaked earlier life, she had certainly found the humble-hearted place by the time I met her.

Like the other Wise Ones, her spirituality was broad and inclusive and all about seeking the Spirit in the now. What cemented her faith, she said, was not holy-nun stuff but broken people who loved her back to life during her own brokenness. It was they who showed her that God actively uses our brokenness to help others who are just as broken. Despite her decades of religious practice, she discovered among these irreligious but spiritual folk that God was within her own heart, not just out there in Heaven somewhere.

There was a depth of wisdom in this woman regarding the path to a humble life, because she had walked it. So, I listened, and the rewards were plentiful. Wise-one stuff ensued that spoke directly to the heart about falling so you can rise, becoming broken before you can really become whole. She spoke about constantly *failing as a prerequisite of real spirituality, not perfection and control.* She said, "On the spiritual journey, we're either in surrender or between surrenders." What a teacher.

CHAPTER TWELVE

EMBRACING THE MANY FALLS

There may be no bigger misconception about the spiritual journey than the notion of perfection. I finished the last chapter with a quote from my favorite ex-drunk nun that is worth repeating: "We're either in surrender or between surrenders." This concept of ongoing surrender, of either being in one or on one's way toward the next, is spiritual wisdom par excellence.

The delusion that somehow those of us who have found a spiritual remedy for our ills are henceforth pretty much perfect is sadly mistaken. We are all subject to plenty of ongoing, self-centered ego compulsions. As stated in Chapter Ten, keeping it real requires that I embrace the many falls that occur as the result of my ongoing struggle with the manifestations of the ego-self.

It is crucial to remember that, above all, it is our brokenness, not our perfection, that makes us most useful to God. Spiritual brokenness produces groans from the soul that cry out to the only source of healing available, the living Spirit that permeates all. Once this healing occurs, we journey with that same living God back out into the bloodied trenches to carry healing to the next sufferer.

Becoming perfect, including spiritually perfect, needs to be taken off the table as a viable option. Perversely, the only thing within us that demands perfection is that selfsame spiritual illness, which simultaneously makes perfection impossible. In the realm of the Spirit, an ongoing struggle is the norm. Indeed, it is the basis for true spiritual progress, which has everything to do with ongoing surrender and nothing to do with being perfect. The solution to the destructive bind of the self-centered ego is not in striving to overcome it but in surrendering completely, letting go of any notion of being perfect.

This goes to the core of what it means to live a spiritual life. We are not just dependent on the living God, who is loving and compassionate, to get us *onto* the spiritual path. We remain dependent all along the way. The beauty within each one of us is now in view. But it does not entirely banish the brokenness of the ego-self to the badlands. Rather, the ego is still very much in the game and ever eager to make a full return. The difference between my former non-spiritual existence and now is not some holier-than-thou place of perfection but a constant need for help with the ongoing ravages of the persistent ego. Experience has taught me it is only the living Spirit who gets to do the healing of the ego thing. Let me be completely clear: there is no magical place where I get rendered white as snow.

To paraphrase Voltaire, perfection is indeed the enemy of the good. Without constant surrender, there is no prospect of arriving at the humble-hearted place, the up-close-and-personal-with-God space. If I'm caught in the delusion of perfection, the good that emerges from repeated falls and the need that follows from them to re-embrace surrender get lost in the mix. Why would the perfect me need to engage with such continual humbling of the ego-self?

Pride and perfection are really just two sides of the same coin because they create the internal lie that either (a) there's nothing to see here because I'm pretty much perfect now that I'm having a red-hot go at the God stuff, or (b) I've blown it again. I should be better than this. I'm not on the spiritual path because I just keep mucking things up! Which is just as destructive to actual spiritual growth.

In my case, there has been a truckload of surrenders along the way. *I'm either in surrender or between surrenders.* Most of them I wouldn't have put my hand up for, at least not initially. But something about the surrender game grows on you over time because the payoffs are huge. These multiple surrenders provide the needed fuel to get to the humble-hearted place. But there's no denying this is hard work; we are talking here about committed spiritual practice, and the very thing that makes us so broken in the first place—the self-centered, prideful ego—resists this with every trick in its extensive armory. The authentic spiritual life rarely, if ever, includes quick fixes. We must prepare for a long walk with plenty of off-track, lost-in-the-forest experiences along the way.

Life would be so much easier if I were just made perfect, if I were to become the recipient of one of those choirs-of-angels, job-done, suddenly-made-perfect experiences I mentioned in Chapter Nine. Over time, though, I've seen that this is just fanciful thinking—where Saint Cormac hovers over the rest of humanity, who are still suffering from the ravages of ego, poor things. Meanwhile, I look on with due sympathy from on high! The problem with this scenario, however, is that once elevated to my coveted saintly abode, I am of no use whatever down here in the broken world.

Again, it is our brokenness, when joined with God's healing, that makes us most helpful to others in the real-deal spirituality of the humble-hearted walk. We will make scant progress on the path to freedom until we embrace this counterintuitive spiritual reality completely. *The spiritual quest is a call to compassion, not separation, and the meaning of compassion is "to suffer with."* This means real empathy by sharing in the suffering that ego produces, not being exempt from it.

Far from saintly, I am a certified expert in having to go back to people to make amends for my frequent misdeeds—heartfelt, humbling recompense to the many fellow travelers who have caught my ire, stirred the old, misdirected passions, and got a good, ego-off-leash, tongue-lashing for their trouble. Every act of face-to-face amends is a propellant toward a humble heart. This essential element of humility, righting wrongs as I continue to run amuck, is an active counter to the prideful ego that vigorously opposes the three hardest words in the English language: "I was wrong." Humility, as a way of living, requires ego-deflation. I have found that few methods are more effective in this essential task than one-on-one, eyeball-to-eyeball admitting that I was wrong.

My problem with repeat offending, as already stated, is the capacity of the self-centered ego to re-manifest almost immediately after every serious surrender. Blink your eyes twice, turn around three times, and the ego is back in business. I recall listening to a speaker many years ago who recounted that, brought to his knees, reduced to a state of almost nothingness, he had subsequently enjoyed eighteen months of complete peace. At that point, he said, "I became somebody again!" What followed was the need for daily conscious surrender for the next sixteen years.[16] So let me say it again: the quest for a humble heart is no quick fix or simple thing. We are dealing here with an ongoing struggle with the most powerful foe that most of us will ever know: the ego within. Even the Wise Ones with their double dose of the Divine also experience the insidious ego; they'd hardly be human if they didn't.

Of course, there is much progress along the way. If that were not the case, I would probably have given the game away long ago. As surrender becomes an ongoing habit, the limitless beauty of the Spirit flows like a mighty river straight into the heart. The deeper the surrender, the mightier the flow. An essential element of this progress is stepping away from perfection as soon as possible and embracing the many falls that come—because come they will. And when they do, will we use them as an opportunity for spiritual growth in humility, or will they become another layer of unresolved spiritual disease?

---

16 Chuck "C", *A New Pair of Glasses* (Irvine, CA: New Look Publishing Co, 1984).

However counterintuitive it sounds, embracing failure and abandoning perfection facilitate an intimate relationship with the living God. Many people genuinely reach for the sunlight of the Spirit only after getting seriously wet with the icy rain of pain. It can't be said too often that the key spiritual paradigm of brokenness is one of our greatest assets, for it is precisely in the broken space that we most fully experience the Spirit doing the healing and humbling thing in our hearts. It doesn't get any better than that!

Embracing the falls also propels me toward the humble action that is required to rectify whatever harms result from my ongoing brokenness. This righting of wrongs is an active and tangible ingredient in attaining the greater humility I seek. It is especially true when accompanied by the full suite of mystic practices referred to earlier in this book.

In conclusion, the humble embrace of spiritual imperfection bears its deepest fruit when I step away from the demand for perfection in others. They are, one and all, fellow sufferers in the spiritually disordered, ego-rampaging journey that we are all on together. Genuine humility of heart is never far removed from cutting some real slack to everyone else on the trek. After all, they are just like me: imperfect. However, this kind of essential empathy will materialize only if we seek it from the source, from the great humbler and healer God who walks with us.

Embrace the falls, dear comrades; they are the cement that binds us to God and makes us especially useful in helping others, who do plenty of falling of their own in this beautiful but broken world!

CHAPTER THIRTEEN

HUMILITY: IT'S A DOING THING

It is well said that "there is nothing new under the sun." This certainly applies to the axiom that humility is a doing thing. One of the most frequently quoted biblical passages about humility is from the Hebrew prophet Micah:

> What does Yahweh require of you? To act justly and to love mercy and to walk humbly with your God. (Micah 6:8)

Every single aspect of this maxim relates to action. There is nothing passive about it; it is the definitive doing-humility prescription.

Micah was one of the out-there prophets in eighth-century BCE Judah. This region was a southern kingdom, formed out of what had once been the territory ruled by the Hebrew kings Saul, David, and Solomon. However, a dismantling of this larger kingdom occurred in 930 BCE, leaving the twelve tribes of Israel divided into two kingdoms frequently at war with each other.

Micah and others like him in both kingdoms were remarkable men who "spoke truth to power." This was a high-risk strategy, and many paid for it with rejection from their communities and even their lives. Calling those with wealth, power, and influence, including the priestly caste, ungodly, faithless folks who should radically change their ways did not make many friends. In the cultural setting of the time, being in relationship with God was synonymous with life itself; it was everything. Overtly criticizing the powerful as religiously flawed was serious business and not for the fainthearted.

In the sweeping biblical narrative of salvation history, the Hebrew prophets repeatedly call the Israelites to return to their core spiritual principles. As God's chosen people, his own cherished nation, they must behave accordingly. Never were they to forget that they were an enslaved people, freed for precisely the purpose of being in a covenant relationship with God and each other. Stratified social structures where power and wealth are monopolized by the few at the expense of the rest were not part of the plan. However, with time, elites always emerge, and inequality and exploitation of the poor become entrenched.

Unfaithfulness to God was and is the cardinal sin for the Jewish people. At the top of the list of infidelities is the worship of other gods. A close second is the neglect of one's neighbor, a theme repeatedly condemned by all the prophets, including the Galilean. It may not seem obvious that Micah's oracle, "Act justly, love mercy, walk humbly with your God," contains all this, but it does. *It is a brilliantly concise summing-up of what it means to be in the humble-hearted space—to be a person who not only believes but entirely depends on God and fully exhibits that through their behavior toward the other, every other.*

Effectively, there are three imperatives prescribed by Micah—justice, mercy, and humility—and they are all *doing* things, not just believing things! All are essential and interweave with each other. Thus, the first two, acting justly and loving mercy, build on each other in order to arrive at the third, the pinnacle, walking humbly with God. This third provision encompasses and makes the first two possible. Walking humbly with God, which specifically denotes God or Spirit reliance, is both the destination and the vital enabler of every stage of this threefold spiritual practice.

There are many paths that lead toward an intimate relationship with God. However, I am convinced this threefold prescription is not only an exceptionally good formula for the journey but also the means of remaining in that space. It is the manifesto supreme in the quest for inner peace and freedom. Let me now try to put some more clarity around what living according to this justice, mercy, and humility maxim might look like. Remember always that these three imperatives are interdependent, and all require real and sustained action to come to fruition.

In Chapter Ten, I wrote about the concept of the inherent dignity of the human person within the purview of Imago Dei (being created in the image of God). That is the benchmark of whether justice is being done to others. For when the meaning of Imago Dei is fully applied, you reach the irrevocable conclusion that *all* life is sacred. There can be no hierarchy according to which one human life is of greater value than another. The underlying implication of Imago Dei is that we are all part of God, and God is innately part of us, in our deepest being and very existence.

The critical point is that acting justly requires each of us to uphold the inherent dignity of the other—every other! *When anyone loses their innate dignity, everyone's dignity dies on the vine,* and restoration occurs only when we unequivocally restore dignity to everyone. The imperative to act justly goes deep. It is a call for restoration of dignity to all. *Anything less just doesn't cut it.*

Regarding the second component of Micah's oracle, "love mercy," the implications are no less acute. I have said much in the preceding chapters about the pervasiveness of the broken ego. By definition, therefore, I am a person in need of constant mercy. It is a spiritual axiom, however, that the Mercy River has a two-way flow. If I want to be a recipient, I must seek a more merciful response when someone else's spiritual brokenness causes me harm. As the receiver of mercy, I should become an active mercy-giver. Now, this is a very tall order indeed. But, hey, no one said this stuff was easy.

Another vital consideration is the translation of the word *mercy*. In Hebrew texts, mercy is inseparable from and often translated as "compassion," which means to suffer with. Seen in this light, *love mercy* would translate as "love compassion," or "love to suffer with." This is not a moot point because it goes to the heart of what is being proposed by Micah. The recipient of compassion or mercy must become an equal giver, someone willing to suffer with the suffering of others. Again, this stuff's not for the fainthearted (more about that in the next chapter).

But there's more. To understand fully what Micah is advocating, it is necessary to comprehend his use of the term *love*. When this word gets penned in scripture, it is most frequently within the context of what the ancient Greeks called "agape," the highest form of love. This is love that is other-centered, self-sacrificing, and unconditional—love that demands nothing in return and persists no matter what the circumstances. Real-time, active love, love as a verb, a doing thing that transcends the sway of the self-centered ego in favor of the other, every other. It is love that is infused with Spirit, without which it is not possible, and from which alone it can manifest. *It is God's love made tangible in humans.* Therefore, when Micah says, "love mercy," he means that mercy must flow freely and without condition—because, like love, from which mercy is inseparable, it is manifestly other-centered.

Again, given the pervasiveness of the ego in us all, neither the "act justly" nor the "love mercy" edict is even remotely possible unless enabled by the Spirit. Thus, both these essentials lead to and depend on the third imperative, "walk humbly with your God."

Walking humbly with your God is an unequivocal embrace of God-dependence. There is a modern parable that may help throw some light on this:

A highly skilled tightrope walker easily makes his way on a tightrope across Niagara Falls, receiving the loud applause of onlookers. For an encore, the sizable crowd are asked to consider if they believe he can make the return crossing while wheeling a wheelbarrow in front of him. All enthusiastically agree that, yes, without doubt, this guy could do it. However, when he then invites any willing spectator to hop into that wheelbarrow for the return journey, not one steps forward.

Walking humbly with God means getting in the wheelbarrow. Otherwise, in the final analysis, I'm really just another onlooker.

After setting out my sorry tale in the first two chapters of this book, in Chapter Four I began to focus on the crux of what had always been the problem: the enemy within, the ego in its various manifestations. Subsequently, I have stressed that in the quest for a humble heart, it is God-dependence, not self-reliance, that I must nurture above all else—because without the living God, who is love and compassion, all bets are off. Micah's third imperative, "walk humbly with your God," is not just an invitation to get into the wheelbarrow but an assertion that no other options are available.

Each phase of Micah's oracle, if fully pondered—whether it is justice that upholds the innate dignity of all or unconditional, love-inspired mercy—falls outside of what we can reasonably expect of humanity if our track record throughout history is any guide. Humility is the apex because not only does it affirm God-dependence but also, in that space, we effectively become a walker with God, a doer with the Spirit, not merely a receiver and onlooker. Ultimately, to act justly, to love mercy, and to walk humbly with your God is to be in the wheelbarrow, way out on the tightrope, becoming a transmitter of the out-there, countercultural, inside-out, radically other-centered love that is God.

CHAPTER FOURTEEN

HUMBLE-HEARTED LIVING BENCHMARKS

The quote from Micah expanded upon in the last chapter is humility par excellence in practice. This is because it expresses not just a necessary reliance on the living God, who is love and compassion, but also, crucially, that such Spirit-dependence must always find tangible expression by being released into the world. As the Galilean says:

> Give and you will receive. Your gift will return to you full pressed-down, shaken together to make room for more, running over, and poured into your lap. The amount you give will determine the amount you get back. (Luke 6:38)

Humility of heart is always a two-way flow. In one direction, there is the lavishness of God's love and compassion that is received. In the other, each recipient heart, now softened, changed, and restored, must emerge as a humble doer. Radically inclusive spirituality must always find tangible expression through the practice of that same love and compassion out in this beautiful but broken world. The supreme spiritual paradox is that what we receive is to be given away entirely. The inward flow must always find an outward expression of doing other-centered justice and mercy through love. Or, as some of my pals on the journey like to say, "You've got to give it away to keep it."

Of course, this is an optimal level of humble-hearted practice. On most days, we all fall far short of this high mark. After all, humility of heart rules out perfection. Serious shortcomings will always emerge in our other-centered love game. This should not prompt a self-crucifying exercise; it is simply an acknowledgment of the role the ego continues to play in thwarting agape in favor of self-centeredness. As previously outlined, this ongoing deficiency, if properly viewed, can propel us toward an ever-deepening surrender or God-sufficiency. This is especially so if accompanied by honestly sharing these failings with others, who've got plenty of failings of their own, and by fast, effective amend-making for whatever ongoing harm has inevitably occurred. Remember, it is only as we walk the broken shore that we learn what God has really got in store for us.

That said, there is a need for concrete benchmarks. I should strive daily toward the higher order of things, and my objectives need to be defined. This could be Micah's threefold prescription or something similar. Most spiritual traditions that have stood the test of time will have within them long-established strands of humility practice that more or less reflect Micah's code for living. Admittedly, these vital threads are often submerged beneath layers of hierarchical, triumphant religiosity, but at their core, most will have the beacon of practicing humility as foundational. Obviously, the practice of humility goes beyond one example from a single Jewish prophet. But whatever the source, definite yardsticks need to be firmly in place. How else do I measure my progress? It is not likely I will get to the top of the humility mountain unless I keep the peak in view.

Equally crucial to the venture, it is worth repeating that ongoing daily meditation is a given. It may not be the Ignatian mystic model discussed earlier in this book, but some form of constant, intimate God-consciousness or Spirit-awareness is essential. It really is all about *seeing the living God in all things!* Nothing is more fruitful for this type of heart-awareness than sticking to it with meditation. Without this as a staple, I am unlikely to arrive at the humble-hearted place or to have much real chance of dwelling there. As previously asserted, in my experience, this is not some difficult, esoteric, otherworldly adventure. It is entirely earthbound and possible for anyone who gives the practice, in whatever form, a persistent and consistent go.

A sure-fire formula for the journey is honestly revealing my failings to others, who also carry the wounds of the broken shore, righting wrongs as they recur, and giving ongoing attention to meditation. These spiritual practices must become second nature for the process to mature. However, ultimately, they are without purpose unless they manifest as wacky, out-there, countercultural, other-centered love. It is not so much the pursuit of happiness that is on offer here, although that is, without doubt, a wonderful side-effect; it is rather the pursuit of usefulness.

In Chapter Two, I said that the two things that I ran hardest from for a good portion of my life were being a servant to anyone and being poor. Eventually, both turned out to be the two things that I must embrace the most. Regarding poverty, there are two kinds that need to be distinguished: material poverty, which is not required but sometimes assists in the journey, and spiritual poverty, which is analogous to God-dependence or Spirit-sufficiency or, indeed, humility itself. This, in ever-growing portions, is indispensable.

Though vital, this much-desired spiritual poverty or humility of heart manifests and grows only when what we receive gets passed on to others in full. *This means the active adoption of servanthood as the definitive marker of my way of being in the world.* Without embracing this other-centered servant role, the inflowing reception of love and compassion from God would be one way and prone to egocentric desire. Servanthood, conversely, is the outflow of what I receive and, therefore, is not only affiliated with humility but is its lifeblood, the very thing that simultaneously enables the inward flood to be vibrant, continuous, and put to right purpose. This correlation can be further extended: the more I become a servant to others through active justice, compassion, and love in the world, the more these same attributes of God flow into my heart. *Where the practice of outgoing servanthood is abundant, so too is the influx of the Spirit plentiful.*

Every teacher referred to in this book, whether personal or in written form, is an exemplar of the primacy of servanthood. Unsurprisingly, given my constant referencing of him throughout these pages, it is hard to go past the Galilean Hasid if one is looking for a supreme historical example of a Spirit-imbued, selfless servant. This God-with-skin-on man lived and died as a humble servant. This is fundamental to everything we can ever know about him. He didn't just teach that being a poor servant to all was paramount; he lived and breathed and was it, writ large. Micah and others like him had the formula and practiced it, but this guy turned it into an art form.

One of the most enduring images that Christians have assigned to the Galilean for the past two millennia is that of a suffering servant. This image, taken from Isaiah (Isa 52:13–53:12), who wrote several hundred years before the Galilean's time, makes for some seriously sober reading:

> He had no beauty or majesty to attract us to him, nothing in his appearance that we should desire him. He was despised and rejected by mankind, a man of suffering, and familiar with pain. Like one from whom people hide their faces, he was despised, and we held him in low esteem. (Isa 53:2–3)

The full quote of the above is the climax of four withering pieces of mystic poetry by Isaiah that highlight the broken figure of the suffering servant, the first three being Isa 42:1–4; 49:1–7; 50:4–7. Contextually, though, Isaiah was not writing about or predicting Jesus per se. Most scripture scholars agree he was writing about Israel or possibly one of the other prophets of his time. But this is a classic case of "If the cap fits, wear it." And the earliest Jewish followers of the Galilean, particularly after his death, found much in Isaiah's suffering-servant descriptor that mirrored their own slain leader exactly. Indeed, given the Galilean's propensity for quoting Isaiah, it is certainly possible these enduring Hebrew texts significantly influenced him in his mission as a model of antihero messiahship (further explained in Chapter Sixteen).

Mercifully, not too many folks, at least in recent history, have had to suffer the same fate as the Galilean in order to follow his example of service. But the cross is profound in its long-standing and wide-ranging symbolic applicability. The suffering-servant model both leads to and extends from the cross—the sort of cross that is sufficiently flexible in its symbolism to include what most people end up experiencing, in one form or another, in this beautiful but broken world.

Embracing servanthood has always been a countercultural endeavor. It makes no sense at all if you're still on top of the heap, flying high. Elites just don't get it, and why would they? To a large extent, we in the West are still subject to a modern version of the honor culture that dates back to the Greco-Roman world. In that world, servanthood was akin to slavery, dishonor, and shame. For the cross of suffering to be willingly embraced was simply unthinkable. And yet it is this very symbol of absolute humility that has, above all, endured as the central emblem of Christianity.

Certainly, for folks across the ages who have spent time on the cross of suffering, who know all about the place of brokenness, who have drunk from the cup of powerlessness, this suffering-servant stuff is not only familiar but sweet indeed. It is not incidental that suffering people from all over the world, including a multitude of oppressed people across the ages, have found great solace in the example of the Galilean. For, as we all know, after the suffering, there comes the rising, the light out of darkness, the new dawn. The dying and rising symbolism of the cross, while obviously pertinent to the Christ, applies to the lived experience of people in every time and place. Not least among these symbolic representations is the death of the ego-self, in order to rise with a new purpose as a servant to all.

The truly remarkable thing about the suffering-servant approach is that when the rising comes—and it does—every aspect of one's suffering energizes and enhances one's servanthood and makes it more useful and compassionate. The crosses we bear become our most useful assets. We must have skin in the suffering-with game, or servanthood cannot reach its full potential.

If or when you get to take a reluctant stroll down the boulevard of broken dreams, you inevitably end up with a close encounter with the cross of suffering. It may turn out, however, that when the rising comes, this suffering becomes a key component of really useful, other-centered, empathic servanthood. *You've just got to have skin in the suffering-with game or else compassion as a doing thing, a humble-hearted practice thing, is just an illusion.* It may be that in this beautiful but broken world, this is the only thing that can make any sense out of our suffering at all. Suffering, my dear comrades, is the mother that produces compassionate hearts, and this is a benchmark you can bet your life on.

CHAPTER FIFTEEN

A TOUCH OF THEOLOGY

I said in the Introduction that I didn't intend to write an academic, theological book. Nevertheless, I have referred throughout to the living God, who is the manifestation of love and compassion, and constantly referenced the Spirit. Also, instead of the more common use of Jesus or the Christ, I have spoken about the Galilean. A context-driven approach underlies these descriptors and the other scriptural references I have included. This chapter will take up these points, all of which are interrelated, and locate them within the purview of academic theology.

In terms of the living God, two theological imperatives are crucial and provide the bedrock of much of what I have asserted. First is the widely accepted idea of salvation history, which I will outline below. Second, more remote but, to my thinking, just as important, is the concept of "deep incarnation." This expresses the radically inclusive presence of God in and through all of Creation. It expands the traditional Christian view of the incarnation event to one having profound salvific reach, not just for humanity but for all life on Earth. God is not missing in action out there in the heavens somewhere. The incarnation of the Christ reflects God being ever-present, not just in a singular reality two thousand years ago but in an ongoing one, with an unlimited reach for all forms of life.

This is the nucleus of the theology behind the "seeing God in all things" Ignatian spirituality that I have embraced. Indeed, my reading of the mystics more broadly suggests that, mostly unrestrained by traditional doctrines, this is the predominant prism through which mystics throughout the ages view their experience of God. In recent decades, under the banner of "deep incarnation," this precept is now also being theologically explored and verified by scholars such as Niels Gregerson, who coined the term,[17] and a wide range of other prominent scholars who are contributors to a recent book on the subject edited by Gregerson.[18] Not least among these is the feminist theologian Elizabeth Johnson, whose scholarly contribution on the subject is robust and inspiring.

My repeated descriptor of God as "love and compassion" is likewise not happenstance. It has a deep theological basis and a consequent biblical underpinning. The source is Exodus 34:6–7, a foundational passage of scripture that biblical scholars identify as a credo that seeks to clarify the core attributes of God. The passage reads as follows:

---

17 Niels Henrik Gregerson, "The Cross of Christ in an Evolutionary World," *Dialog: A Journal of Theology* 40, no. 3 (2001): 192-207.

18 Niels Henrik Gregerson. *Incarnation on the Scope and Depth of Christology* (Minneapolis, MI: Fortress Press, 2015).

Yahweh passed in front of Moses, proclaiming, Yahweh, Yahweh, compassionate and gracious God, slow to anger, abounding in love and faithfulness, maintaining steadfast love for the thousandth generation, forgiving iniquity and transgression and sin, yet by no means clearing the guilty, but visiting the iniquity of the parents upon the children and the children's children to the third and the fourth generation. (Exod 34:6–7)

What makes this passage so profound is that it is a declaration from Yahweh (God) specifically outlining what God's character is like and thus how God behaves in this world. This prompts Mark Boda to assert that Exodus 34:6–7 "is clearly a moment of divine self-disclosure on a level that transcends any other revelation."[19] In theological terms, its importance can hardly be overstated, precisely because it is so often quoted in Hebrew scripture. A creed is a micro statement that contains the core beliefs expressed in the wider body of writing. Exodus 34:6–7 has this creedal status because of the multiplicity of its use in other biblical texts. The inclusion or echoing of this declaration about God's love and compassion occur in biblical literary contexts encompassing *narrative* (Num 14:18–19), *sermon* (Deut 5:9–10; 7:9–13), *psalm* (Ps 86:5, 15; 103:8–12; 145:8–9), *prophecy* (Joel 2:12–14; Jonah 3:10–4:2; Mic 7:18–20; Nah 1:2–3), and *corporate confession* (Neh 9:17–20, 31–32).[20]

Without doubt, the element of God's wrath is also reflected in the credo and thus repeated in some passages that mirror

---

19   Mark J. Boda, *The Heartbeat of Old Testament Theology: Three Creedal Expressions* (Grand Rapids, MI: Baker, 2017), 35.

20   Gordon R. Clark, *The Word Hesed in the Hebrew Bible* (New York: Bloomsbury Academic, 2015), 247-52.

or directly quote it. But proportion here matters because the emphasis is almost entirely on God's love, compassion, and willingness to forgive. Expressed numerically, this is a thousand in favor of love and compassion, as against a tiny, almost nonexistent four in favor of wrath.

As is always the case with scripture, context is vital because what is being conveyed in terms of God's wrath is not my childhood perception that God really, really doesn't like bad boys. Instead, wrath—both in the Exodus narrative and thereafter—is a response to ongoing betrayals of the covenant relationship between God and the Hebrews. What is being narrated in the section of the Exodus story where the credo occurs is that God's chosen ones have just broken a covenant established in Exodus 19:1–24:18. The behavior in question that drew God's ire is apostasy, the worship of other deities (Exod 32:1–6).

Later in Israel's history, the prophets will repeatedly point to apostasy and the almost-as-egregious sin of acting unjustly to the poor as examples of covenant violations. God's care for the poor and consequent expressions of wrath or justice-seeking when the poor are mistreated play an important and positive role in covenant theology. This concern finds full expression in many of Israel's covenantal laws. When making loans, the Israelites cannot charge interest to the poor (Exod 22:25). When rendering judgment, no distinction is to be made between the rich and the poor (Exod 23:3; Lev 19:15). Deuteronomy 15:11 exhorts that "Since there will never cease to be some in need on the Earth, I therefore command you, open your hand to the poor neighbor in the land." The Hebrew prophets—including Isaiah 3:14–15; 10:2; Jeremiah 5:26–28; Ezekiel 22:27–29; and Amos 5:11–12—explicitly condemn those who neglect or oppress the poor. Yahweh's special care for the poor is also highlighted in the book of Psalms (68:10; 72:13–14; 112:9; 113:7; 140:12). The poet who penned Psalm 146 captures this brilliantly:

> Happy are those whose help is the God of Jacob, whose hope is in Yahweh their God, who made Heaven and Earth, the sea, and all that is in them … Yahweh executes justice for the oppressed; gives food to the hungry; sets the prisoners free; opens the eyes of the blind. Yahweh lifts up the bowed down; loves the righteous; watches over the strangers; upholds the orphan and the widow. (Ps 146: 5–9)

Every part of Hebrew scripture, and indeed the New Testament, gives expression to God's care of the poor, hungry, or oppressed. When this is ignored by omission or commission, the covenant is in breach, and thus, God's wrath, the need to seek justice for the poor, gets activated.

In the ancient world, covenants are binding treaties between rival kingdoms. These agreements were of the highest order, taken extremely seriously, and breaches of them would elicit severe punishment.[21] The covenant analogy to regional treaties is important because in that cultural setting, the dire consequences of breaching a covenant were inescapable and fully understood by all. Seen in this context, God's response to the violation of the covenant in Exodus 32:1–6 is even more extraordinary. Because rather than inflicting a just punishment, one that would be violently forthcoming in the human realm, the penalty is proportionately so minuscule

---

21 William J. Dumbrell, *Covenant and Creation: An Old Testament Covenant Theology* (Milton Keynes, England: Paternoster, 2013), 126-129.

that it becomes all but insignificant. In fact, rather than exact an appropriate penalty, God immediately ratifies a renewed covenant in Exodus 34:10–28.

It is specifically this context that always needs to be brought to the fore when dealing with the many instances of wrath language that are deployed in the Bible. The Hebrew prophets, both major and minor, certainly emphasize God's wrath. But this is always in response to what they believed had either already befallen or was likely to occur as the direct result of the Israelites' running afoul of covenant observance. If the poor get oppressed or apostasy occurs, the covenant with Yahweh gets smashed to smithereens. That said, the critical thrust in prophetic writing—and indeed in scripture more broadly—is that after the wrath, because God's inherent nature is love and compassion, without exception there always comes a time of redemption.

The concept of salvation history mirrors the trajectory of the repeated rise and fall of the Israelites. Both rising and falling in the broader narrative are inseparable from a covenant relationship with Yahweh. Where there is rising, it is because of the intimate favoring by God of the descendants of Abraham through covenant. And when the falls occur, it is in biblical terms because they have broken that relationship. Salvation history reveals that despite constant breaches of covenant, God's true nature as steadfast love and compassion, as revealed in Exodus 34:6–7, is enduring.

We, the children of Abraham, keep smashing the covenant, while God keeps picking up the pieces and offering yet another renewal. These biblical covenants are first between God and all humanity (Gen 6:18); then, subsequently, between God and the world through Abraham (Gen 15:18); God and Israel (Exod 24:1–8); God and King David (2 Sam 7:1–29; 23:1–5); and finally there is the declaration of a *New Covenant written on the heart* (Jer 31:31–34).[22] This is the covenant to end all covenants, penned by the prophet Jeremiah after the mass enslavement of the Jews and the destruction of Jerusalem by the invading Babylonians in 586 BCE.

Jeremiah's covenant of the heart has deep and abiding implications for how Christians see their covenant relationship with God, and it is alluded to or directly quoted in several Christian texts, including in the letter to the Hebrews (Heb 8:8–12). Walter Brueggemann makes the astute observation that the Book of Jeremiah is demonstrative of a twofold movement "into the abyss and out of the abyss." That's what befell the Israelites during Jeremiah's life and is therefore foremost in his writing. However, this twofold movement, into and out of the abyss, falling and rising, also finds full expression in the New Testament. Hence, the theological drama of the Babylonian exile, of displacement and restoration, of falling and rising, gets easily transposed in Christian testimony into crucifixion and resurrection.[23]

Into the abyss and out of the abyss—this is the grand narrative of not only the Israelites but all of humanity, and it finds expression in salvation history. But make no mistake, God's essential nature as love and compassion revealed in Exodus 34:6–7 always wins the day. Even if, as the exiled

---

22 Dumbrell, *Covenant and Creation*, 7.

23 Walter Brueggemann, *The Theology of the Book of Jeremiah* (Cambridge: Cambridge University Press, 2006), 191.

Jews in Babylon could attest, that day seems a long time coming, it always comes. The living God, who is love and compassion, always renews the covenant of the heart. This is salvation history's grand narrative.

Theological inquiry has a very long history; its breadth and depth are extensive. So too are the many methodologies that underpin its academic disciplines. Few things are more fundamental to sound theology than understanding the context of scripture. Without this important starting point, the true significance and meaning of any scriptural passage are likely to be elusive or, worse, receive an interpretation unrelated to its original intent. This requires a detailed study of the text, or what theologians call scriptural exegesis. It usually involves a three-part examination of the text in question, including an analysis of "the world behind the text," "the world of the text," and "the world in front of the text." It is my exposure to this sort of academic work, known as the historical-critical method,[24] that guides the scripture references given within this book. More broadly, I use a method known as narrative criticism, pioneered by Robert Alter in the early 1980s. It seeks to expand the horizons of biblical scholarship by recasting the Bible as a work of literary art.[25] This includes recognizing the wide-ranging use by the biblical narrators of poetry, metaphors, myth, symbolic imagery, and climax, all interwoven into one grand narrative about the salvific God. These are among the methodologies

---

24 An extensive overview of this method can be found in David R. Law, *The Historical-Critical Method: A Guide for the Perplexed* (London: Bloomsbury Publishing Plc, 2012).

25 Robert Alter, *The Art of Biblical Narrative* (New York: Basic Books, a Member of the Perseus Books Group, 2011).

used in mainstream Catholic and Protestant theological scholarship, which rejects a literalist or fundamentalist interpretation of scripture as lacking in vigor and erroneous.

Using "Galilean Hasid" to describe Jesus throughout this book is an adherence to context. Geza Vermes, a distinguished Oxford scholar, first coined this descriptor in his book *Jesus the Jew* in 1973. Although the Jewishness of Jesus may seem obvious from any reasonable study of him, it was an idea that revolutionized New Testament studies in the 1970s, given that many Christians had lost sight of, or downplayed, this stark fact about their leader. Vermes and the many scholars who have subsequently followed his lead seek to place Jesus in his proper historical context as a covenant-observant Jewish outlier from Galilee, a holy man, a charismatic teacher, and healer, a Spirit-imbued God-man (Mark 1:9–10; Luke 4:18; Isa 61:1–2; Matt 12:18; Isa 42:1–4; John 1:32, 3:34). Indeed, a rule-breaking rebel whose interpretation of covenant and teaching of the same is entirely consistent with the love, compassion, and justice-seeking zeal of the God who so thoroughly enveloped him. Here was a prophet in the long lineage of Jewish prophets whose central concern was covenant relations with Yahweh, but one so Spirit-infused he could proclaim, in line with Jeremiah 31:31–34, that this same Spirit was open to all in a new state of being and doing he called "kingdom come" (Luke17:20–21).

The Galilean embodied God's Heaven on Earth vision and mission for the world—one that upends the status quo of unjust hierarchy and privilege in favor of agape love, compassion, and justice. This is a kingdom that begins with transformed hearts, sufficiently humbled so they can perceive the radically incarnate presence of God within themselves and all things. A kingdom, still in the making, of God-dependent, Spirit-enabled, inside-out, upside-down, last-is-first, other-centered love. This is the theology that permeates the quest for a humble heart.

Chapter Sixteen

The Biblical Case for Humility

Come to me, all you who are weary and burdened, and I will give you rest ... For I am gentle and humble in heart, and you will find rest for your souls. (Matt 11:28–29)

Gentle and humble of heart—now, that's exactly the game we're in! We want nothing less than the gold standard of hearts on offer, a humble heart like the Galilean's. This is the promise of all promises, held out to those who make the quest. And yet, concise as this statement is, more scriptural depth is needed to grasp its implications fully.

The case for humility is more easily made from Christian scripture than from its Hebrew forerunner, as I will discuss below. However, the larger body of Hebrew text influences the content of the Christian Bible substantially. The writers of the New Testament constantly reference and quote the Jewish text throughout—not to mention the fact that if context is to be adhered to, the Galilean and all those immediately connected with him were Torah-observant Jews.

Regarding the prominence of humility in Hebrew scripture, one could say it is a mixed bag. There are direct references to humility, including "He mocks proud mockers but shows favor to the humble and oppressed" (Prov 3:34). Indeed, this passage is quoted directly in the New Testament (Jas 4:6; I Pet 5:5). Nonetheless, the use of the word *humility* in general in the Hebrew text is sufficiently scarce that, at first blush, it may seem its centrality is lacking. However, a more careful interpretive lens reveals the opposite. Consider this passage from the book of Numbers, for example: "Now, the man Moses was very humble, more so than anyone else on the face of the Earth" (Num 12:3). In terms of importance for the Israelites, Moses is arguably unsurpassed. And to describe him as the humblest man on Earth puts humility in very fine company indeed. The scribes' purpose in connecting Moses to humility is not opaque. Their purpose is to show that if humility is the defining virtue of Moses, it should be our foremost aspiration as well. If humility is good enough for Moses, hailed as perhaps the prophet supreme, the biblical inference is clear: humility ought to be embraced by everyone!

If the example of Moses' humility is not convincing, there's much more! Some of the learned rabbis from the rabbinic tradition postulate something truly extraordinary: that humility is an essential feature of the character of God. According to the Jewish Mussar tradition, which dates back to tenth-century Babylon, rabbinic scholars have long pondered the implied humility of God in the Genesis narrative. Of particular interest to these learned folks is the following:

Then God said, let us make humankind in our image, according to our likeness. (Gen 1:26)

The specific words in this profound biblical passage that have driven such venerable inquiry by these rabbinic men for more than a thousand years are "let us," and "in our." The point they have extrapolated is that God, who is beyond all and creator of all, is entirely inclusive and communicates with other created life, most probably angels, in the grand plan to create human beings. A little caution needs to be exercised here. We do not want to get caught up in the banality of biblical literalism. This is not a debate about whether angels exist; that would be to miss the point the narrator of this version of Genesis is trying to convey. There are no throwaway lines in scripture. Here, the author is framing Creation as a collaborative venture in which God includes and consults with other created entities before creating humanity. This says something vitally important about the character of God. *The conclusion of the learned rabbis, although the text does not overtly say it, is that what is being expressed is that God is humble.*[26]

This same sentiment about God's humility is further captured in the prophetic writing of Zechariah 9:9–10, in which a humble messianic king brings peace to Earth (also quoted in Matt 21:5; John 12:15). Now, if one accepts that the creator God is humble, and one of God's most esteemed servants, Moses, is the humblest man on Earth, and if the depiction of the messianic king is similarly humble, it's easy to see why humility has received a lot of attention by the rabbis. Collectively, these insights are highly significant because what they suggest is that *humility is not only prominent in the*

---

26 Alan Morinis, "Occupying Your Rightful Space," in *Humility: The Virtues,* ed. Jennifer Cole Wright (Oxford: Oxford University Press, 2019), 25-30.

Hebrew text but ought to be the central defining virtue of all those who seek God. As Isaiah says:

> For thus says the high and lofty One who inhabits eternity, whose name is Holy: I dwell in a high and holy place, and also with those who are contrite and humble in spirit, to restore the spirit of the humble and revive the heart of the contrite. (Isa 57:15)

Yes, the most-high God dwells with and gets drawn toward humility of spirit and contrite hearts, perhaps because these traits reflect the very best of humanity when mingled with the humble character of God. This may well be one of the most important insights in this book: *like does indeed get attracted to like, love to love, compassion to compassion, and in this case, innate humility to unending depths of the same.*

One further point needs to be addressed before moving on to discuss humility in the Christian text. Textual scholars of Hebrew identify that the words "poor" and "lowly," which are copiously used throughout the Bible, have interchangeable meanings. In one sense, "poor" or "lowly" can mean materially poor, and this is consistent with what Western readers understand "poor" to mean. However, in the Hebrew text, "poor" or "lowly" very often translate as "poor of spirit" or "humble in disposition" and "God-dependent." Therefore, when the words "poor" or "lowly" receive the correct translation in the text, "humble" is sometimes being implied and at other times "materially poor."[27] Although the words "humble" and "humility" are not frequent in English

---

27   Sue Gillingham, "The Poor in the Psalms," *The Expository Times* 100, no. 1 (1988): 15-19; Stephen B. Dawes, "Humility: Whence This Strange Notion?," *The Expository Times* 103, no. 3 (1991): 72-75.

translations of the Hebrew Bible, the use of the words "poor" or "lowly," which imply humility, is copious. Hence, even though the English translations rarely identify it, the inference of humility can be made throughout the text. While not obvious at first, humility is a deeply embedded imperative in Hebrew scripture.

In Christian texts, humility as a primary virtue is front and center. However, what makes it so is the imagery—drawn substantially from selected Hebrew texts—used to tell the story of the Galilean. As noted above, the humble messianic king from Zechariah 9:9–10 is an image used by some of the Gospel writers to depict the humble messiahship of Jesus (Matt 21:5; John 12:15).

Likewise, it is difficult to discern anything other than humility from the "suffering-servant" moniker, so often applied to the Galilean, which, as we've seen, finds its source in Isaiah 52:13–53:12. That so many of the New Testament narrators would settle on this suffering-servant image to describe the Galilean puts humility at the epicenter of the Christian story. Just how central is the focus of many scholars.[28]

My study of the texts and the accompanying scholarship suggests that the suffering-servant imagery and the consequent humility that it invokes, while not the only image in the New

---

28 William H. Bellinger and William R. Farmer, *Jesus and the Suffering Servant: Isaiah 53 and Christian Origins* (Harrisburg, Pa: Trinity Press, 1998): Bernd Janowski and Peter Stuhlmacher, *The Suffering Servant: Isaiah 53 in Jewish and Christian Sources* (Grand Rapids, Mich: William B. Eerdmans Pub, 2004).

Testament pertaining to the Galilean, is the most pervasive. The extent to which the Galilean himself was aware of and modeled his journey on the suffering servant will never be fully and definitively known. But without doubt, his followers, particularly after his death on the cross, certainly saw this suffering-servant exemplar as depictive of him. As also noted earlier in the book, this was a case of "If the cap fits, wear it." What needs to be grasped, however, is that this humility cap pertains not only to the Galilean. *It is the humble, thorny crown that has to be worn by all those who claim him, both then and now.*

The suffering servant's back story provides the context for many of the sayings attributed to Jesus about humility. As noted, he refers to himself as "gentle and humble of heart" (Matt 11:28–29). But it is clear that his followers, likewise, must embrace humility above all. This was and is a very demanding, life-changing, countercultural proposal. But consider the following directives from the God-man:

> The greatest among you shall be your servant. For whoever exalts himself will be humbled, and whoever humbles himself will be exalted. (Matt 23:11–12; 20:25–27)

> Whoever wants to be first must be last of all and servant of all. (Mark 9:35; 10:43)

> But you shall not be like them. Instead, the greatest among you should be like the youngest, and the one who leads like the one who serves. (Luke 22:26)

> No one can serve two masters; for he will either hate the one and love the other or be devoted to the one and despise the other. You cannot serve God and Mammon! (Matt 6:24; Luke 16:13)

The parallels between these various utterances, often recurrent within one Gospel—and repeated throughout the other Gospels in ways that are strikingly similar—give them considerable weight as authentic teachings of the Galilean. Equally authentic is when the disciples get sent out on missions. Their marching orders are to emulate their leader as penniless, itinerant folk, with all the attendant suffering implied. "He instructed them to take nothing but a staff for the journey, no bread, no bag, no money in their belts" (Mark 6:8; Luke 10:4; Matt 10:9–10).

Palpable in all this prescriptive teaching is that the humble suffering-servant life, devoid of power, prestige, and money, underpins it all! Small wonder he had far more listeners than people prepared to get in the wheelbarrow out on the tightrope. Make no mistake, this is the program outlined by the God-man, the humble modus operandi he offered to those willing to walk the talk of humility. This is the roadmap to Damascus, where the keys to the kingdom get discovered. *The suffering-servant life, the real-deal* path to inner peace with purpose. And it's all laid out in the Christian text.

Similarly, it is clear from the New Testament letters of St. Paul, who was writing well before the Gospel passages quoted above, that he explicitly saw the lineage of the humble suffering servant as not only applicable to the Galilean but also to himself and all those who claim the Christ.[29] Indeed,

29 Otfried Hofious, "The Fourth Servant Song in the New Testament Letters," in *The Suffering Servant: Isaiah 53 in Jewish and Christian Sources,* eds. William H. Bellinger and William R. Farmer (Grand Rapids, Mich.: William B. Eerdmans Pub, 2004), 163-188.

as Reinhard Feldmeier argues, "Paul established a direct relationship between humility and the Christ event, thereby making it an ideal of Christian ethics."[30] Humility was so central to Paul's theology of the cross that his writing became the nucleus of its transformation from a negative term into an enduring Christian ideal.[31] As Paul says, "Do nothing out of selfish ambition or vain conceit. Rather, in humility value others above yourselves, not looking to your own interests but each of you to the interests of the others" (Phil 2:3–4). And finally, in parallel to Paul and with no less emphasis, the author of First Peter echoes his Israelite forerunners: "All of you must clothe yourselves with humility in your dealings with one another, for God opposes the proud but gives grace to the humble" (I Pet 5:5; Prov 3:34).

Part of the enduring literary genius of the Bible is that diverse themes are brilliantly woven through this vast, spiritually compelling treatise. Humility in practice is certainly not the only theme on which biblical scribes seek to shine a bright light, but without doubt it is a central and ongoing one.

---

30 Reinhard Feldmeier, *Power, Service, Humility: A New Testament Ethic* (Waco, Texas: Baylor University Press, 2014), 61.

31 Feldmeier, *Power, Service, Humility,* 62.

CHAPTER SEVENTEEN

IT'S ALL ABOUT THE HEART

It is reasonable to ask why I have placed more emphasis in this book on the heart than on the mind. The brief answer is that, in the end, the *language of the heart, which is love, is where all the action is.* Not that I want to belittle the magnificence of the mind's capacity for reason, the accompanying amazing progress of the sciences, or the brilliance of philosophical thought; the world would certainly be much the poorer without them.

But the ascent of the age of reason has been so unadulterated and complete that we in the West, especially, have long been prone to a kind of all-encompassing mind warp. So focused are we on all things of the mind that the ancient wisdom of the heart gets relegated to some barely visible status. This explicit focus on the mind is fertile ground for the ego-self and what some folks now call "the Me generation," and a fella like me knows all about that. I want to make the case that this unhappy circumstance, if not wrong-headed, is certainly wrong-hearted.

My point here is not to deny a central role to the mind and indeed the body but to re-elevate the heart to its former glory as king of the heap—the number one go-to place for the thing that is most precious in life; the thing without which it is hardly a life at all, the ineffable thing that we call love.

The language of the heart has never been entirely remote. God alone knows how many writers and poets, indeed artists of every ilk, have toiled at their noble trade, keeping it alive and projecting its vast and inscrutable depths right back at us. For it is from the heart that love metaphors plentifully abound; it is the heart alone that is the vital receptacle of love. These creative folk give voice not only to the joys of love but also to its crushing encounters. Eventually, the vicissitudes of life guarantee that everyone gets a dreaded taste of what that feels like—when love gets shattered, denied, lost, or fractured beyond repair. Or the barren despair and desolate state of hard-heartedness, where love neither enters nor thrives or completes its vital journey as other-centered outward flow.

Love's radical highs and desperate lows are the most pervasive currency the world has ever known! Every creed and culture, every time and place, knows of its incredible joy and heartbreaking loss. For love, we will weep and mourn, on the one hand, and on the other, overcome insurmountable odds to glimpse and receive its gentle touch. It is love that makes us fully human, and love that is the essence of God. *When these are bound inseparably as one, the quest for a humble heart is in full swing. For it is only in the heart where this happy union with the Spirit occurs.*

A friend of mine likes to quote an old priest whom she heard say, "God is the energy of Love." Could this be the stardust from which we all come, the essential kernel of life itself? I think it could be. The second account of the Creation story in the Book of Genesis says that God breathed the breath of life into humanity and thus created human beings (Gen 2:7). *It is entirely consistent with everything else that unfolds in the Bible to suggest that this breath of life, this life-giving Spirit, is the beautiful-beyond-belief, strange-yet-somehow-deeply-familiar, known-but-never-fully grasped thing that we call Love.* All the great mystics eventually arrive at this conclusion.

The author of the Gospel of John, sometimes called the fourth evangelist by theologians, says it all definitively in one of his letters:

> Let us love one another, for love is from God, and whoever loves has been born of God and knows God. Anyone who does not love does not know God, because God is love. (1 John 4:7–8)

To be in the God game is to be in the love game! Any perversion of this is just that, an unfortunate perversion. And if love is the game, then the heart is the center for action because from it all transmissions flow. Mind stuff is fine and dandy and, without doubt, required. But in the end, it's the heart, the heart, where all the spiritual action goes down!

The ancients understood this only too well. They may have lacked our modern advances in physiology, but regarding the centrality of the heart and its connectedness to love and thus God, they have much to offer to our mind-centric world. For them, the heart offered not just a bodily organ essential to blood flow but a spiritual center of existence on which all else depended. Jan Bovenmars captures a contemporary vision of this insight:

The heart is the wellspring of life. The heart indicates what is present and living in the depths of a person. It refers to the origin of what we feel and think, of what we decide, say, and do. The quality of a person depends on the quality of their heart.[32]

As already stated, it's not that the mind and body don't equally matter in the totality of our spiritual existence. However, the heart is the central driver of our existential self. And it is so precisely because it is so identifiable with the wondrous, mysterious energy we call love. When we talk of love, we think of the heart. This connection is innate and gets used extensively by storytellers, including the scriptural scribes. For in matters pertaining to life and love, it's the heart stuff that really matters. If the heart is in good shape, so too will love and life be.

The reverse of this heart fitness, or sound heartedness, holds equally true. Although time and cultural context produce variants, humanity has always been subject to the things that block or direct us away from our best selves, our heart-centered, God-connected, love-infused selves. Marcus Borg, for example, in writing about the Galilean, asserts:

Jesus saw people as profoundly selfish. Concerned above all about self's well-being and security and seeking that through the means offered by culture. The primary allegiances cultivated by conventional wisdom are ultimately pursued for the sake of self in order that it may find a secure home in them.[33]

---

32 Jan G. Bovenmars, *A Biblical Spirituality of the Heart* (Staten Island: New York: Alba House, 1991), Preface.

33 Marcus Borg, *Jesus A New Vision: Spirit, Culture and the Life of Discipleship* (Sans Francisco: Harper & Row, 1987), 107.

If this focus on self-centeredness was what the Galilean observed in first-century Palestine, it is not a stretch to say that it is matched in every other time and place, and it certainly holds true for a fella like me. This is the overarching concern of the grand narrative of the Bible: hearts gone astray in pursuit of the wrong goals. Hardened hearts enslaved by self-centered desire, hearts that urgently need a good shake-up, a large dose of salvific love, a complete transformation and restoration.

The heart as the epicenter of life gets mentioned over a thousand times in scripture. In some contexts, the reference is to the literal bodily organ (2 Sam 18:14; 2 Kgs 9:24; Tob 6:5; Ps 45:5). However, far more often, "heart" is used metaphorically to mean the emotional core or the seat of life (Prov 4:23; Mark 7:21–23; Luke 6:45). Heart is used to describe the spiritual, ethical, condition of a person (Ps 24:4; 73:1; Prov 22:11; Mark 7:21; 2 Cor 5:12). The heart displays happiness and joy (Prov 15:13; Ps 16:9; 33:21; Acts 2:26), sadness and grief (Ps 13:2; Prov 14:10, 13; 15:13; Acts 2:37), and fear (Ps 27:3). God can scrutinize the heart and discern what lies within (Ps 17:3; 26:2; Jer 12:3; 17:10; Luke 16:15; Rom 8:27; 1 Cor 2:9–10). But God can also transform the human heart and cleanse it (Deut 30:6; Jer 4:4; 24:7; 31:33–34; 32:39; Ezek 11:19; 36:25–26). In the New Testament, a change of heart gets stressed (Gal 4:6; Rom 5:5; 2 Cor 3:3; Heb 8:8–12; 10:16; cf. Jer 31:31–34). And God sends the Spirit into the heart to do just that (Gal 4:6; Rom 5:5; 2 Cor 1:22).[34]

---

34 Scott Hahn, *Catholic Bible Dictionary*, 1st ed. (New York: Doubleday, 2009), 346-347.

You could say that the Bible is all about the heart. While it is certainly possible to do plenty of theorizing and study of God with the mind—and this is all to the good—experiencing the living God is another thing entirely. This well and truly falls into a different sphere: for this, you've got to get into the heart zone, the Spirit realm, the mystic space.

I mentioned in the Introduction that arguably one of the greatest exponents of Christianity who has ever lived, Augustine of Hippo, famously said, "Our hearts are restless till they find rest in thee." We are built for this restless quest because our hearts are designed to yearn deeply for the love from which we come. But it's the now-stuff of the heart that really matters. The breath of life, the Spirit of God who is love, is deep within us; it whispers to us gently, creating a yearning for an ever-deeper, intimate connection with this love. It's just that this ancient wisdom of the heart gets lost along the way by worldly clamors, religious elitism, self-centeredness, pride, and suchlike.

Earlier, I wrote about Jeremiah's covenant of the heart, and it is not incidental that it is among the references to the heart just listed. Jeremiah was writing about an exiled people taken into slavery by the Babylonians, a scattered nation that had lost the very core of their spiritual world with the destruction of their temple in Jerusalem. He offered the banished Israelites new hope by drawing deeply on Hebrew tradition and envisioning something far grander than any external temple before or since. What Jeremiah saw was God's temple in our hearts, and the ethical code or covenant of love that is written deep within.

Perhaps the wackiest and most out-there of all the prophets was a fella called Ezekiel, also referenced above, and he had this to say:

> Thus says Yahweh ... I will sprinkle clean water on you, and you will be clean; I will cleanse you from all your impurities and from all your idols. I will give you a new heart and put a new Spirit in you; I will remove from you your heart of stone and give you a heart of flesh. (Ezek 36: 25–26)

It just doesn't get any better than this. If the old heart is flaky through misadventure and dysfunction, there's a bright, shiny new one on offer that leaves the old one for dead. And yes, it gets infused with a double dose of the same Spirit of love and life that God breathed into humanity from the start! The same Spirit the Galilean would later proclaim as not only the all-encompassing beat of his own heart but the only game in town for one and all.

Once, a really smart fella, as really smart fellas are wont to do, came to the Galilean with a tricky question. He wanted to know if Jesus could summarize all the great teachings in the first five books of the Bible, known as Torah law (Mark 12:28–31; Luke 10: 25–28; Matt 22: 34–40). Now, the Galilean did what holy men are inclined to do. He reached deep down into the depths of his own tradition, pulled out two gems, and then joined them together as one: "Love God and love each other" (Deut 6:4–5; Lev 19:18). In the final analysis, that says it all. That really is all there is. When you peel back the all-and-sundry, you end up with "Love God and love each other;" you end up in the quest for a humble heart. For what on earth could be more humbling than the boundless mystery of God's love and the endless adventure of embracing the same in the heart? *It's all about the heart* because it's all about radically inclusive other-centered love. In the end, that's all there is. For when the heart gets changed, everything changes.

Not everyone needs to be brought low, shaken and stirred, and reduced to a state of powerlessness and despair to find the path to inner peace and freedom.

But I did!

Bibliography

Alter, Robert. *The Art of Biblical Narrative.* New York: Basic Books, 2011.

Bellinger, William H., and William R. Farmer. *Jesus and the Suffering Servant: Isaiah 53 and Christian Origins.* Harrisburg, PA: Trinity Press, 1998.

Boda, Mark J. *The Heartbeat of Old Testament Theology: Three Creedal Expressions.* Grand Rapids, MI: Baker, 2017.

Borg, Marcus. *Jesus, A New Vision: Spirit, Culture, and the Life of Discipleship.* San Francisco: Harper & Row, 1987.

Bovenmars, Jan G. *A Biblical Spirituality of the Heart.* New York: Alba House, 1991.

Brueggemann, Walter. *The Theology of the Book of Jeremiah.* Cambridge: Cambridge University Press, 2006.

"C.," Chuck. *A New Pair of Glasses.* Irvine, CA: New Look Publishing Co., 1984.

Clark, Gordon R. *The Word Hesed in the Hebrew Bible.* New York: Bloomsbury Academic, 2015.

Dawes, Stephen B. "Humility: Whence This Strange Notion?" *The Expository Times* 103, no. 3 (1991): 72–75.

Dumbrell, William J. *Covenant and Creation: An Old Testament Covenant Theology.* Milton Keynes, England: Paternoster, 2013.

Feldmeier, Reinhard. *Power, Service, Humility: A New Testament Ethic.* Waco, Texas: Baylor University Press, 2014.

Gandhi, Mohandas K. *The Collected Works of Mahatma Gandhi.* Vol. 31. New Delhi: Government of India Publications, 1961.

Gillingham, Sue. "The Poor in the Psalms," *The Expository Times* 100, no. 1 (1988): 15–19.

Gregerson, Niels Henrik. "The Cross of Christ in an Evolutionary World." *Dialog: A Journal of Theology* 40, no. 3 (2001): 192–207.

Gregerson, Niels Henrik. *Incarnation on the Scope and Depth of Christology.* Minneapolis, Minnesota: Fortress Press, 2015.

Griffiths, Bede. *The Golden String: An Autobiography.* Springfield, Illinois: Templegate Publishers, 1954, 1980.

Hahn, Scott. *Catholic Bible Dictionary,* 1st ed. New York: Doubleday, 2009.

Hofious, Otfried. "The Fourth Servant Song in the New Testament Letters." In *The Suffering Servant: Isaiah 53 in Jewish and Christian Sources.* Edited by William H. Bellinger and William R. Farmer, 163–188. Grand Rapids, MI: William B. Eerdmans, 2004.

Janowski, Bernd, and Peter Stuhlmacher. *The Suffering Servant: Isaiah 53 in Jewish and Christian Sources.* Grand Rapids, MI: William B. Eerdmans, 2004.

King, Mary Elizabeth. *Mahatma Gandhi and Martin Luther King Jr: The Power of Nonviolent Action, Cultures of Peace.* Paris: UNESCO Publishing, 1999.

Law, David R. *The Historical-Critical Method: A Guide for the Perplexed.* London: Bloomsbury Publishing, 2012.

Morinis, Alan. "Occupying Your Rightful Space." In *Humility: The Virtues.* Edited by Jennifer Cole Wright, 25–40. Oxford: Oxford University Press, 2019.

Nouwen, Henri J. M. *The Wounded Healer: Ministry in Contemporary Society.* New York: Doubleday, 1972.

UN General Assembly. "Universal Declaration of Human Rights." 217 (III) A. Paris, 1948. https://www.un.org/en/about-us/universal-declaration-of-human-rights

Vermes, Geza. *Jesus the Jew: A Historian's Reading of the Gospels.* London: Collins, 1973.

Williams, Rowan. *Silence and Honey Cakes: The Wisdom of the Desert.* Oxford: Lion Books, 2003.

Wilson, Bill. *Alcoholics Anonymous: The Story of How Many Thousands of Men and Women Have Recovered from Alcoholism,* 4th rev. ed. New York: Alcoholics Anonymous World Services, 2001.

About the Author

Cormac Stagg is a Christian mystic, poet, public speaker, and author. He completed a Bachelor of Theology at The Australian Catholic University. A survivor of both alcoholism and ongoing depression, he has walked the walk of committed spiritual practice for more than a quarter of a century. Writing from the heart about radically inclusive spirituality, he lives near the back of beyond with a reformed alley cat who has never befriended another living soul.

More at cormacstagg.com

Printed in Great Britain
by Amazon